Praise for The Jeshua Collective

I am overwhelmed with tears of joy at the information that was given to me about my mother. I have found someone that I can trust with readings.

Jeshua Collective validated my mediumship abilities and walked me through what was happening with my own awakening. I was afraid of what was happening, I no longer feel paranoid. I am looking forward to the future instead of dread. It is heartwarming to know I have abilities. Thank you, Jeshua.

Jeshua is undeniably speaking through Carol. She (they) knew things about my life that is not on social media or available publicly. I am able to heal myself from my past and their guidance is undoubtedly the reason why.

I was hesitant to get a reading over the phone about my loved one, but within the first thirty seconds there was information that came through that was incredibly accurate (personality traits, physical issues, and words spoken before he passed). I am eternally grateful for finding Carol and her guides.

I wanted to truly thank you for such an amazing I AM weekend. I am beyond grateful for having the opportunity to receive healing from Jeshua and to also embrace new life experiences that were much needed for me. My heart is overflowing with tears of joy as I move forward in my life. I cannot thank you enough!!

All I can say is I hope I never miss an opportunity to attend the I AM Intensive weekends. I feel different, less stressed. Things just don't bother me anymore. I'm working on bringing my husband to one of them!

I can't thank you enough for what you do. The world needs to know the ACIM study group Spiritually Led Journey exists. Of all the ACIM groups I've belonged to, none have brought channeled conversation from Jesus to it to answer my questions. I feel blessed to have found you, Carol. Thank you for what you do.

Carol, I feel so blessed to have found you. The channeled reading I had with you changed my life. You are the real deal.

Thank you, Carol, for a great healing of my dad's condition. He felt better immediately. I'm happy for the serendipity of life's unfoldment.

Manifestation
OF THE TRUE SELF

A Guidebook For
Believing in Your Ability to Self-Heal

———— Self Healing Series ————
Book 1

CAROL COLLINS
Original Channel for The Jeshua Collective

Manifestation of the True Self
A Guidebook for Believing in Your Ability to Self-Heal

Copyright © 2022

All rights reserved. No part of this book may be reproduced by any method for public or private use–other than for "fair use" as brief quotations embodied in articles and reviews–without prior written permission of the publisher.

The intent of the author is to provide general information to individuals who are taking positive steps in their lives for emotional and spiritual well-being. If you use any of the information in this book for yourself, the author and the publisher assume no responsibility for your actions. Readers are encouraged to seek the counsel of competent professionals with regards to such matters.

Powerful You! Publishing is committed to publishing works of quality and integrity. In that spirit, we are proud to offer this book to our readers; however, the story, the experiences, and the words are the author's alone.

Published by: Powerful You! Inc. USA
powerfulyoupublishing.com

LCCN: 2022922152

Carol Collins – First Edition

ISBN: 978-1-959348-05-4

First Edition December 2022

BODY MIND & SPIRIT / Channeling & Mediumship

Books Written by Jeshua

<u>Channeled Works</u>

Ocularity of the Mind: Ocularity Series, Book 1 (2022)
Mind Body Connection: Mind Body Series, Book 1 (2022)
Manifestation of the True Self: Self Healing Series, Book 1 (2022)

<u>Contribution</u>

Women Living In Alignment (2022)

At this publishing of this book there are fourteen additional works that have been channeled and are in queue for publishing, with more on the way. To stay in contact with us, please subscribe via the website:
www.thepittsburghmedium.com

Dedication

Jeshua, thank you for all you do for me and all your students. I love that your methods and terminology are unique and uniquely designed to improve intuitive abilities. Little by little, Grids are cleaning up—thanks to you.
It is the secret to law of attraction.
I love you for teaching this through me.

To all of my dear readers – I hope you receive clarity from Jeshua's teachings and that the logic, the visual descriptions, and the storytelling means of teaching helps you as much as it has me. I have great love for all of you. The following is for your reference:

Parent Soul Being is the individual pea within the pod construct,
the outer ring of a tree trunk construct,
and the newest pearl on a strand construct.

Stream of Consciousness is the Higher Self
and the set of peas in a single pod construct,
the entire strand of pearls construct,
or the full set of layers of the tree trunk construct.

When the Higher Self grows to a certain size
and makes certain decisions, it can accumulate
the entity Being title by creating more like itself;
and, they are a part of you, as you are them forever.
You are one.

Table of Contents

Books Written by Jeshua	v
Dedication	vii
A Pillar 3 Book	x
The Essential Material	xi
Introduction	xiii
Chapter 1 ~ Clarity	1
Chapter 2 ~ Influence	11
Chapter 3 ~ Conveyance	25
Chapter 4 ~ Imaginativeness	37
Chapter 5 ~ Connection	47
Chapter 6 ~ The Changed Person	73
Chapter 7 ~ Recognition	95
Chapter 8 ~ Purification	105
Chapter 9 ~ Free Flow of Ideas	115
Chapter 10 ~ Cleansing the Root Chakra	125
Chapter 11~ Grounding Explained	133
Chapter 12 ~ Uprooting: Root-Cleansing Activity	141
Chapter 13 ~ Running the Energy: Root-Cleansing Activity 2	151
Chapter 14 ~ Directing Energy Maintenance Sequences	159
Chapter 15 ~ Quantity-less	175
Chapter 16 ~ Stoppage Indicators	183
Opportunities to Engage with Jeshua	191
About the Author	195

A Pillar 3 Book

*Dictation received in channeled state in
November 2021, captured in 14 video-recorded
sessions, spanning 4 consecutive days,
for a total of 9.5 hours.*

The Essential Material

The Four Pillars of Learning

PILLAR 1: The Foundational Material - The starting point for understanding who "Source Beings" are, who we are, and why we are having this life experience.

PILLAR 2: Idea Reconstruction - Otherwise known as law of attraction, deliberate creation, verbal therapy, and using the power of thought energy to manifest your life, on purpose.

PILLAR 3: Directed Energy for Self-Healing - Moving Source Frequency within "the grid" as a means of clearing unconscious beliefs that stop and/or delay your ability to connect with your Guide team and manifest a life of abundance.

PILLAR 4: Intuitive Development - Verbal and vibrational instruction to open your inter-mind to ocular (mind's eye) to increase your ability to receive, clarity in that receiving, and accuracy on what your Guide is conveying to you.

Introduction

Session: 1, video #0701
November 17, 2021

We are Jeshua to speak. Those among us have begun to write, as we said we would, through this woman, Carol. We said we would before she was born. One of us did and now we all do. The first two books planned for her beginning have been completed, and this one will not only add to it but explain some things that so many of you have been wanting.

The only thing you need to know is that we are Real; everything else is a bonus. Who are we? We are a collective of Beings that have a similar focus. Through Carol we teach The Essential Material—The Four Pillars of Learning. She is the one that we have identified as being able to allow us to teach some on all of these subjects. We have much to teach you, and much of it will be in book form. We gather together as a collective, we teach as a collective, and we individually contribute to the overall message of The Essential Material. Some of us teach classes and write books; others teach classes only, for that is what we have chosen to do. We are Beings in the nonphysical and so are you—but you are not presently aware of it. We are. We are The Jeshua Collective. You may call us a Council if you like. It is also accurate to do so.

This book is number three in the order that they were written. It is good to read them in that order. It is also Book 1 of a third series, and it was written by one of us. We do not always identify ourselves as the book-writer or teacher because you, dear ones, get too anxiety-riddled when we do.

We are love. Carol enjoys the term Love Beings. I like that. Who am I? Antioch (An-tee-aahk). I am older than all here, but my Beings, the lifetimes, and the entities that bore them are not as learned as I am because they have not begun the training in all of the areas that I have. That is the way of it. They do, however, write as well. When we write through a person, or teach, as the case may be, we draw upon Higher Beings, or our own Teachers at times to provide you with the material that is desired.

We are loving Beings. We share freely, we want you to learn to as well. I write this book and more will come because Carol's High Guide asked it of me. It is good for the development of her Higher Self. I am author of this book and yet I am not, for we all contribute. The gatherer of the material is an entity within my Being and we are happy to call it an Antioch book for it was written by one of us. But it is also a Jeshua Collective book because we care not about ownership. You do. We love Jeshua Collective. We are Jeshua Collective. We are Love Beings.

There are things that I, my Greater Being (or "myself," for ease of explaining this to you) want you to know specifically. There are also things that we, Source Beings, nonphysical Life Beings, want you to know. There is also The Collective of Jeshua and the teachers within and among us that I draw upon, for The Collective has specific teachings that we plan to do through Carol.

It is good for you to let go of your identity while you read channeled works and realize that we teach you (nonphysical Knowing) to guide your lives. You do not know us, but we know you. I know Carol and I know who she is becoming

Introduction

in the nonphysical. She is one of mine that I teach. She is, and her High Guide as well, in my care. They are assigned to me and that is why I am here. If she were aligned to another, another would be here teaching the same or similar material because it is the guidance given for her Soul Being.

Your lives are much more important than you realize. Your life in the physical is important to us. You are not aware of the greatness that your lives contribute to the overall Being that you really are. Failure is not failure to us. Failure is choosing to start in a different place after becoming a physical being than you identified for yourself prior to becoming the human being that you are. It is a different starting place. That is all it is.

Do not subject your minds to believing that negative emotions are real. They are a misunderstood vibration within the inner psyche of your Being. This statement is explainable and I am hoping that you will feel your way to creative questions so that you uncover Knowledge.

I speak in general terms so the population learns our ways of teaching. It is for consistency, however, for there is always more to learn! And there is always more to teach. I love this opportunity to guide you in ways that I have not yet done. Self-healing is an art form of living in the physical world. It is creative play of thoughts plus emotions plus Knowledge plus action. It is good for you to engage with us as we teach in person. It is good to ask questions so we can guide you individually. It is good to broaden your knowing and the knowing of others. It is one of the reasons you have been drawn to us as your Teachers.

I want to describe something so that it is not misunderstood.

I am an entity, which means that I have branches before me and after me. In the nonphysical, if you have a series of lifetimes, you are a Being. I am an entity which is an accumulation of Beings and individual lifetimes, as well as nonphysical experiences that are separate from human incarnations. There are many entities within my Greater Being and I am the Greater Being for many entities.

There are many such Greater Beings within and/or among The Jeshua Collective. We are a subcommittee of the committee of Beings that have risen to the level of committee members. I like that analogy. We are allowed to be on as many subcommittees as we choose, for it is what we do—we teach. Each subcommittee has its own human channel. That is that. I hope it makes sense to all of you now when you hear us say, "We speak through this channel only." When another comes along, we regroup, reform, re-committee ourselves based on the Unfoldment Plan for that person and the information that we plan to teach. And we can and do teach through many people for your benefit.

My description of entity is rather simple to understand. You have an arm and a leg and fingers and fingernails and toes and toenails and ligaments and eyelashes. It matters not if you name each part individually—you have them. Same thing. There is a Being who once upon a time decided to have lifetimes. That Being is the original, and that Being decided to, at one point in time, create another like itself. It is something we all do.

There is an original Source of Life for my Being, although there is also not. The way we describe it makes it appear linear, but that is an oversimplification and phrased this

Introduction

way to create understanding. Your world works off of linear time—days, weeks, months, years, twenty-four hours in a day, followed by another day and another day and another day and another day, and so on.

In the nonphysical dimension, there are no days. There are also no nights per se. There is timelessness and being who and what we are. My Being was created by its own Parent Soul Being and it was created by a different yet connected Parent Soul Being. I too have created my own (bore my own) Parent Soul Beings, who would be able to create lifetimes in the physical world. I am an entity because of it.

Where does a family begin? You have a parent, you have siblings. Your parents had parents and they both had parents and they both had parents, and they both had parents. It is not dissimilar to your own genealogy, yet it is because it is not siloed. It is not genetic-based. It is Love that multiplies. We are intelligence of a type and that is all—intelligence of a type. There is also no opposite of us. We are purity of love, just love—and intelligence. Add those two things together and what do you get? The same two things, just more of it. I want you to know that this is who we are, as well as what we are, and that you are not unlike us.

Currently, you are having a physical life experience. Many of us have completed doing that and no longer participate in that activity. We could if we wanted to, but we do things differently. You will as well at some point in your own nonphysical development. What do I do? I create. I observe. I assist. I teach. I speak through this woman, Carol, now. I want you to know that these things that I say are not my opinion. It is not my perspective. It is the Knowing of Source

Beings, of which I am one. That part of you that is still participating in nonphysical-dimension-type activities is like me, but not as broad or deep in its knowledge. That is "the why" for you having a physical life experience and me having completed them.

Your lifetime is valued by All That Is. It is valued by your Higher Self. It is valued by that Being that is you. Understand this a bit more clearly—you are imagining yourself in a world so clearly, so deeply, so intently that the characters of your imagination feel as though they are real. It is like having a thought that can think. It is exactly like having a thought that can think because that is what is occurring.

You are a thought and you are thinking. How can a thought think? Because it was created for you to be able to do so. We are not mere human beings in invisible form. We are powerful, as are you. What we do is different. What we have available to us is different because we are not in physical form. You will have these things available to you as well when you are fully here again.

The capacities are different between us. You have some, we have all. You have much, we have much, much, much more. You have more than you realize. Some of you are attempting to do things like astral project and prepare your minds for out-of-body experiences (OBE), but you also say things like, "Where's my paycheck?; "I want to buy it on sale."; and "Don't go down that street in the dark."

You have created your own limitations. You have created your environments. You have created your lives. You have created your bodies. You have created your mannerisms. You have created your personalities…almost.

Introduction

There are aspects of you that are what we call built-in. Those aspects (traits, if you like that word better), were hand-selected to form the basis of your human experience. You are living a physical life experience, but it is a perceived experience that you yourself is having. You do one at a time and you keep doing them until you have completed what you set out for yourself to do: learn how to be in that perceived place and feel peaceful and react and respond in a peaceful way. More specifically, until you have stopped accumulating stoppages in your Root chakra, until you have purified your physical form, mostly.

There are some things that can be done in the nonphysical dimension rather than the physical worlds. That is the only reason I say mostly. You do not know what your inner-mind (substitute ego mind) does with everything that you look at, take in, ingest, et cetera. Sometimes it ignores what you are doing, lets it slide. You get a hall pass. Other times, you do not. It is as if there is a watchful eye at every corner in the hallway and you get detention left and right. That is coagulation of thoughts.

You get caught again and again and again. When you get caught enough times on a certain type of thought or a certain type of emotion, then the mind, the inner part of it, learns something about you and then creates it as if it knew what you were trying to do all along.

For example: "I'm trying to write my name. I'm trying to write my name. I'm trying to write my name. I'm trying to write my"—and your inner-mind then catches on and says, "Oh, you're trying to write your name. I'll do that for you, thank you for letting me know," and then you have difficulty doing things yet you learn to write your name. You get both because you created both. The inner-mind snatches the baton from you as you are trying to work through a situation and gives you what you were thinking about. Fun, is it not, to learn this? I hope so, because we are teaching it this way again and again. We teach using storytelling; it helps your inner-mind learn what it did wrong so that we can re-teach it to create properly.

Now, this inner-mind, it does not snatch the baton every single time. That is what creates frustration for you. Not for us, because we see what the mind is doing. We watch it. We see what is accumulating. We form a plan to help you. You do not see what is coming. We do, and we keep you steady emotionally when you allow us to.

Who is meant by "we?" In this instance it is The Guardian—your Guardian, specifically and individually. When I say we throughout this book it also means The Jeshua Collective and/or Consciousness Beings at large. I want you to understand a little more about your physicality so you can hear us.

Now, let's get on with it. Thank you, Carol.
Introduction complete. November 17, 2021, 9:30 p.m.

CHAPTER 1

Clarity

Your Soul Being that resides in a dimension where you are not is thinking at this moment and they are thinking you into being.

Chapter 1 ~ Clarity

Session: 2, video #0702
November 17, 2021, 9:35 p.m.

It is November 17, 2021 at 9:35 p.m. Carol likes when I say this at the beginning of the video. She has an annoyance to deal with when she listens to it afterwards when I do not. I think she needs to lighten up on it. She does not yet choose to. We have an agreement now, or at least most of the time, that I will comply. Why do I comply? Because during one annoyance moment she looked up and to the right, as she always does when she speaks to me, and asked me to do something instead of simply focusing on the annoyance. She asked me for help.

She likes to label things with the date. The time is a memory-marker but useful, so I give it to her. She records herself as I speak through her and then uses an internet site for auto translation of the video. She listens and reads simultaneously, line by line, word by word, phrase by phrase, correcting errors in punctuation as she goes. It is not a difficult process, but it does have some bumps here and there.

Know that when I say it has some bumps here and there, I am not influencing her mind nor helping her to miscreate. I have to be able to use examples; otherwise, how would I teach you how to have a better life? You need examples. Am I planting a seed in you that grows into something that you do not want? No, because I will not allow it. How can that be? What am I doing? I am doing something that I know how to do. I speak to you vibrationally so as to not add quantity because of the words I choose. I also teach you verbally to heal yourselves.

To teach you, I speak through a human being. Not ocular speaking, but out loud speaking the way we do through a channeler. What does ocular mean? Clairvoyant. The word is overused and it also is too watered down—clairvoyant, clairsentient, clairgustation, claircognizant, clairaudient are the terms you often use. You use them incorrectly, as we taught you in the last book. I teach you this to give you an opportunity to learn from us and so that your inner-mind learns as well. It is preferred for you.

What is a clair? Clarity. Clarity of the mouth, clarity of the taste buds? It makes no sense to the inner-mind—it does not teach the mind what it is supposed to do, in other words. Clarity of the nose, clarity of aromas, clarity of the eye, clarity of seeing. Some people say mind's-eye sight, seeing in the mind's eye. Some people use the same phrase "mind's eye" to describe their own thinking thoughts, their imagination. The problem is that people do not know for sure if his or her thought was imagined.

I like to say, are you certain it was not received? Because I want you to consider the idea. Where do your ideas come from? Where do your thoughts come from? Some come from the inner-mind, the part of you that you say thinks. I say, "retrieves." You have the ability to retrieve thoughts as well as receive them. If it is received, then it means the inner-mind was handed a thought from someone else. Who is that someone else? Your High Guide, your Guide, your Guardian. It is useful to know that the terms I use are many. That is how we all teach in The Jeshua Collective so that you connect the dots with the variations that are available to you by human straightforward teaching.

Chapter 1 ~ Clarity

I describe for you now The Guardian. They are a collective of nonphysical vibrational Beings that have formed together in unity for the preservation of your physicality, for observation and tending to your life path. It is a big job. I teach not just the definition of the term through this woman, Carol, but I teach it—meaning I teach entity Beings how to become it! Those that are doing it in the nonphysical had to learn from someone. That someone is me or others like me. I teach High Guides how to do what they do. It is not the only thing that I do, but it is one thing that I enjoy very much. I will continue doing it until I decide to do something different.

Some of you believe that you have a Guide or a Guardian. Prepare yourselves for this—you do! But it is more than that. It is not one person. Sometimes people say, "My grandmother passed and she's now my Guide." It is never the case. She might become a Helper. She might choose to participate in your life from the nonphysical place that she is now in, but she is not your Guide (capital G) because you already have one. You have to have one in order for you to take your place inside the human body.

I talk about auras. I talk about energy fields. I talk about physicality. I talk about Guardians. I talk about Source Beings. I talk about human beings and why you are having this life experience to some degree, and how to enjoy it to a large degree, by way of self-healing. The Guardian is not one Being. It is a collective formed to guide you into, during, and out of physical life. I describe first beings, then branches of beings, entities, parents, all beings and parent entities.

A Being begins as a thought. If that thought, or if it is

recommended for that thought, to have substance then it takes form and becomes a Being. When that Being is fully formed, it has life. It learns, it grows, it does things—one of which is have physical lifetimes. An extension is a Being who has lived long enough and learned enough to decide that it wants more balance or more of something—or wants the experience of creating a Being. This is always done with their own larger entity Being, because we draw energy from it.

We are not creating a person, not a human being. We are creating a Being in the nonphysical. We are creating a Love Being—a consciousness Being. A nonphysical vibrational Source Being. A conscious Being. Then that Being opens itself up to the knowledge of who it is and starts its ascension process. What is an ascension process? Substitute "learning"; it is a learning process.

When a limb on a tree is strong enough and has enough nutrients within it, when the circumstances are just right, a nub forms and the nub grows into a twig and the twig grows into a branch and somewhere down the line that branch—if all things are right for it—a new nub grows and the process continues. It is the same, more or less. An extension of ourselves.

When a Being is formed it begins its journey of learning, of doing, of being. An extension is like the tree branch. It is where it came from, its Source of Life. That branch came from a branch, which came from a branch, which came from a branch, which came from a branch—and we all come from the same tree.

"Tree of Life" is a beautiful expression. Who is the trunk? Love. It is not a Being per se; it is a quality, and the quality

Chapter 1 ~ Clarity

is whole and complete.

We all stem from love. We all grow from love. We expand love. We expand what we are. We are love. Where we live is whole and complete…just love.

Your physicality is something that we do as Beings. We have physical experiences because our minds can create them, can participate in them. We can band or join together and co-create experiences. That is why you are in a world where there are people, not a world where there is a person. We do that too. But that experience is not a world, necessarily. We focus our imagination so concretely that what we see has depth. Our imagination then has substance. It has qualities. It has aspects.

Your imagination is shallow in comparison when you are a physical person. When you are not, you create as I have described above. You might see an image; it might appear to have depth, but it is still an image, a drawing or rendering. Even if it moves it is not a thinking image. Ours is.

You are it, the one that is having the imagination session. It is you, along with your Parent Soul Being. You are doing it together and your Parent Soul Being can do more than one at a time. You cannot while you are you (physical person) however, when you are a nonphysical Being you will have abilities that match your Parent Soul Being.

The Being that is you in the nonphysical is your Parent Soul Being. It belongs to a Higher Being that is also participating in your physical life. You will always be you, even when you become a nonphysical Being. You are who you are now. You do not die! You will add on to you. You will never subtract from you. The next you will be you plus the next you (next incarnation), and then more. You will continue to grow for as long as you continue to do the activity of having physical lives.

Then you will do something else if you choose to. You never stand still; you never get it done. You always choose something else, but not always right away. There is no ruler on the back of the knuckles if you take your time. And if you take your time, there is a reason for it and your reason is good enough for everyone. We do not argue. We do not mumble. We do not cower. We do not create error. We do not make mistakes.

You, dear one, were thought into being. No matter what your circumstances, no matter where you came from, who you are now, or where you are going. You are not a mistake. You are not an error, and you are good.

It is important for you to read the above paragraph twice but I leave it up to you, and I do not ask Carol to type it out twice. Will you do it? If you believe that I am Source and that these words are being given from an identity that is not Carol's, then you might. If you find value in the words, you might. There is no guarantee because, where you are, you have choice. Get rid of the words "free will" and just substitute "choice." You have choice.

We have choices, but they are elevated choices (because we are nonphysical Beings and when you are as well you will too), and we never, ever, find fault in any of them. We simply choose the one that we are drawn to and we do it. Liken it to your intuition if you want to. It is not that, because we always know the next step in our beingness. It is not intuition because we are not being given the path. Your

Chapter 1 ~ Clarity

intuition is given. You are being given the path, or part of it, or something to get you back on it. We are holy, if you prefer that term. Some of you do. I like pure or purity. They are good words to describe us. To describe all of us.

I want you to have this basis of information so when we describe the physical body and how to heal it your mind knows where the information is coming from and believes— or begins to believe.

You are taught many things from people. Much of it is error because the thinking thought that is you can error. You do error. What is the thinking thought that I say is you? Your Soul Being that resides in a dimension where you are not is thinking at this moment and they are thinking you into being. They are thinking you into being. They are thinking as you are living. They are intuiting to you their thoughts. You are intuiting to yourself. You are thinking yourself through life and intuiting to your perceived being which is you. They are thinking, so you are the thought. You are an intelligent thought, a creative thought that can think. You believe that you are the thinker. You are, but it is not the you that you think. It is the Greater Part of You. You are the physical expression of their thought. They are the one thinking you into being.

If you can understand that, then the rest of this book will be a breeze.

End chapter.

CHAPTER 2

Influence

*You believe us to be vibrational Beings
that give you answers, predictions,
foretell the future. We can and will,
but our job, our function, is to tend to the world.
We are stopping you from becoming
a hateful race of people—genetically.*

Chapter 2 ~ Influence

Session: 3, video #0703
November 18, 2021, 3:30 p.m.

Here we are, November 19th, about 3:30 in the afternoon at the cruise port in Tortola, British Virgin Islands. Carol is sitting in her stateroom. She had a nice day. We went shopping together. What did we buy? Jewels—the necklace kind—and quite a few of them. She planned to purchase three but she ended up buying four, plus another four inexpensive, non-gaudy gems to hang down. They are very pretty. It is what she wants to do, buy jewelry from a jewelry store. Therein lies influence.

You cannot get away from it, but I do like it when you try. So when you are out buying things, look around. Do the opposite of what you would normally do, at least sometimes. Do you look at the sale rack? Do not. Do you look at price tags? Do not. Do you shy away from speaking to anyone about what you like? Do not. Do you meander about, hoping that no one will talk to you? Do not. Stand upright, seek out an attendant or cashier, for that is all they are. They are a cashier in a store. They do inventory. They put tags on. They put items in a case, perhaps instead of hanging them or fold them on a rack. Do the ones in jewelry stores get paid more? Probably. Do they like it? It depends on the day.

Do not let them intimidate you. They might have a dress and jewelry or a suit on. They might have an air of authority while you are in blue jeans and a t-shirt. Do not let it bother you. If you want to look at the merchandise, look. I want you to talk as though you own the place. "I don't want that one. What I want is something a little smaller, a little more delicate. If you don't have it, just let me know I'll find something else." I do not want you to say, "Excuse me, do you have anything that is smaller? I'm not sure exactly what I want and I think I like smaller. I think maybe I don't know what I want. I'm just going to look." Completely different personas.

Influence from the world is not what I am wanting you to succumb to. I do want you to be influenceable from us as Teachers. I know that when you are reading this book, it is not exactly the same as if you were listening to the video. Perhaps the video will be available. I do not yet, at this moment, know if it will be, however, Carol does want all of the audios to be available. I like that so that you can hear the delivery. I have not yet built-in pacing to influence further, although there is conversation about doing just that. If it occurs, we will let you know at the beginning of the book or identify how you can download it and listen at your leisure.

What is pacing? It is when I identify who will be listening to the audiobook, if it were available. I identify the number of years that will be projected for and then together we, as The Jeshua Collective, will identify the proper pace and pauses and begin.

Who am I? An entity among The Jeshua Collective. I like teaching you, I have done so in the past. I do want more books in the world that have been written by Source, written by nonphysical vibrational Beings. Whether they are mine or others like me matters not. Carol's mind likes me—her mind, her inner-mind, the ego mind. Why does it like me? It is attuned to the material.

Chapter 2 ~ Influence

She likes vibrationally-written books, meaning dictating works from Beings like us. Carol herself knows that all Beings in the nonphysical dimension understand physicality and non-physicality, what physical life is all about, and could explain it backwards and forwards and upside down. Her inner-mind is attuned to me, however. That means that when it wants information on this topic, it slows its own thinking down when I am the weaver of the information and hand it to the mind. It listens to me. I stand out from the Collective, as there are many of us in the conversation. Let's put it this way: her mind likes when I do the handshake.

Picture a room full of speakers. Everyone is writing their best work down, putting it in order. I am the one—the tail end, the front end, whichever way works for you—who takes the compilation, hands it to the mind and requests that each word be said in a row. Why me? Because I am doing what I agreed to do. Carol's mind is doing what was built-in for it to do: recognize me and focus on me.

I stepped forward from the Collective when it did, and in so doing I am able to be the individual author of this book. I like it that her mind recognized my signature energy. It is a phenomenon of the mind that did not have to occur, but it did. There is a recognition step that others must do before writing and speaking through her that I do not need to do. You do not see this happening nor hear it in the videos.

When we teach Unfoldment or other classes they are different each time, or can be, because each day is different. The human beings that show up are different, but even if they are the same human beings week after week they are different each and every class session. We also know how to teach the same subject in innumerable ways.

If we want to teach your mind to blink, we could give you a thousand exercises. The same goes for your intuition, increasing your ocular skill level. Whether your practice sessions are alone, whether you are accompanied by one or amongst many or are indoors or outdoors, they all make a difference. The latter is more challenging unless your mind is one of those that is already quiet. If so, then it needs a little more variety to be present. For most of you, you already have too much variety and so you need the opposite. You need a different situation for the mind to acknowledge change. That is where we step in.

Generally, however, humans en masse have minds like robots or computers. They have an on/off switch; you wake up, it is on, you fall asleep, it turns off. I want quieted minds where the light switch is right on the cusp of off so that at any moment we can speak to you. You feel the air around your face, neck, perhaps the shoulders change because you have shifted into a different dimensional place. It is not a different dimension per se, it is a dimensional place within the dimension that you are in. It is a system of dimensions.

This thing that you call a "4D world" is a workable phrase. It is not exactly the way you perceive it to be because you are living your own dimensional life. Some of you are at the bottom end, closer to 3D and others are beginning to move to the three-quarter mark towards 5D. Those are the very gentle ones. Gentler still is where the world is going.

You are on your way to everyone shifting over the precipice, and it is a *precipice*. One by one, you shift into the next dimension. It will not happen while you are in the

Chapter 2 ~ Influence

physicality that you are currently in. But you can shift yourself upwards within these layers, within the dimensionality that you are in currently. It is good to do that.

It is good to do meditation. It is good to listen to channeled works, because when you do your mind understands one thing: a human being did not write the words. You might not know it consciously. You might open *A Course In Miracles*, for example, and you might read it cover to cover, not knowing that Helen was not the authoritative author. But your inner-mind does. Energies are weaved into the book. Vibrationally accurate, they are. Channeled works all have this. They all do. It is what separates a channeled book from a human-made book. You do not know how to weave the energies to impart Knowledge or a message into the vibrational element of the words themselves.

No matter the publisher or the printer—the energies are within the words. If you have an opportunity to listen or watch the video or audio of this recording or others, then you are receiving the same. We breathe through a human being—we say that sometimes. What is really happening is this: the energies have to be combined and Knowledge is inserted. Before spoken through the person, conversation is included because we must soothe the mind of the channel first. We have to say hello so the mind allows conversation from us, and then the weaved message is given out loud to you.

We are gentle Beings. Your mind is not. We have to remind the mind every time that we are gentle Beings. The mind will allow conversation when we do that, so we always do. We have healing that can be built-in. We have influence that can be built-in. We have a gravitational pull, more or less, that we can build in, et cetera, et cetera.

If you want to write a book, do so. Use common sense, however, and write a book that will not only satisfy you and your need to write but one that is good for the world to read. Horror, gore, killing, cannibalism, sacrificial lambs are not good for the mind to take in. There is no creativity in those stories. There are thoughts that came from the world only and we do not condone any of it—not because we are judgmental, but because it harms your internal mind.

You are gentle beings by nature, hidden or masked underneath because of fantasy, war, good-better-best. "My parents didn't have it, so I can't, either" or "Come hell or high water, my parents didn't have it, but I sure as hell will." There is anger in each one of those. We do not want you to become an angry race of people and there are indicators that you could have been. We did not allow it, nor would we. You do not know what we do. You believe us to be vibrational Beings that give you answers, predictions, foretell the future. We can and will, but our job, our function, is to tend to the world. We are stopping you from becoming a hateful race of people. Genetically. This book and those like it are one way that you are being changed for the better.

There are still flare-ups, far too many, of hate and discontent. The flare-ups are within each individual. They spark another, but they cannot create it, they cannot make it. They cannot make you angry if you were not angry to begin with. These angry sentiments or flare-ups within others cannot do something new to you. But they can push your buttons to the point where you allow emotions to rise

Chapter 2 ~ Influence

to the surface. It is rising to the occasion in a bad way that I am referring to.

When that happens, what do you do? The general population does nothing. What can you do? You can learn Directed Energy to self-heal. It is built-in for you to do so. Built-in. It is desired that more of you learn it then share it, believe in it, and do it.

It can heal your life, it can heal your body, it can heal your emotions. It is the missing link that all manifestation gurus have been searching for to make manifesting easy for all. There is such a question mark on how to manifest easier, more consistently. We see it. We love it. We are answering you. Why does law of attraction work randomly? Why does law of creating work randomly? Why? Because of the Root chakra. Because each one of you have different stoppages and the ones that you have are for different reasons.

How do you get something? Let's go through the process. Decide what you want, number one. Add to the idea, some generalities to enhance your love for it, number two. Acknowledge your Guide or Source or whatever word you prefer as your co-creator, your partner-in-spirit because it is always with our help that you get the good stuff, number three. Stay with it—your half of the bargain is staying as positive on the topic as possible, number four. Stay with it longer, number five. Push through the hard stuff and choose positivity on purpose, number six. Continue more on both of these, number seven. You have manifested that thing that you asked for, or enough of it that you are feeling satisfied, number eight. Allow new ideas to form, change your idea significantly, do something completely different, or add on in a way that is significant, number nine—and if you do, you are back at number one.

You have a lot of number one ideas. When an idea comes to mind and you love on it for half a day and then forget about it, it is still a number-one-stage idea. How do you move it to number two? Create a habit to think about it and when you do stay as close to the original idea as possible. If you change your idea too often in the beginning, then you simply have two different number ones and the mind does not know which one you are wanting. The original idea can have some depth to it, so do not get overly cautious. Play with the ideas and then make a decision and stay with that decision.

Your High Guide does know what you are wanting. They do know all the ins and outs. You do not have to write it out to the nth degree. It is helpful to allow an idea to blossom before you alter it so that you can work through the process and see the evidence of it coming. Here is why: Your mind simply gives you things. That is the job that it has assumed. It is the gift-giver, only it does not know good from bad, happy from unhappy, love from hate, gentle from rough. But you do.

You are not your ego mind because you are the thinker. You have the advantage but you do not use it, or at least not often enough. The ego mind categorizes—as I have said, labels—identifies how many labels to make, and then creates a new quantity, always more than the last.

Because of those quantities, your life is what it is. You change your thoughts, the ego mind changes with you. If you are understanding these words, look at your life. Where do

Chapter 2 ~ Influence

you see a high concentration of quantity? If you decide that you want the opposite, or you know you want the opposite, and you decide to do the work, the verbal work, you do have to stick with it. But know this: quantity of light and airy are easy to come by. Stay on topic, stay happy, stay positive, and quantity accumulates. As it does, negative quantity becomes less in comparison.

You have a bag of jellybeans. You no longer want to offer jellybeans to your friends but it is all you have, or so you think. You remember in the back of the cabinet there are M&Ms. It is a pain in the neck to get to the back of the cabinet; you have to move things out of the way, it takes time. But if you do it, you will get the bag of M&Ms and bring them forward. Then you have one bag of each.

If you are loving all over the M&Ms and not the jellybeans, you have more M&Ms coming. You will have less jellybeans coming because the mind will put a pause button on what you do not want if in the moment you have found a substitute. That is good news. So, whenever you are having a thoughtful moment that does not feel good, change it up. Do the flip flop. Back it up to the place of feeling good. Find a substitute, a different topic to think about.

Loving on the M&Ms is similar to shining a spotlight on them. You could put both bags next to each other and the M&Ms have a spotlight when your company comes over for dinner. They automatically choose the M&Ms. Some will not even have registered that the jellybeans were there.

This is an analogy, of course, for your inner-mind and what you are focused on. The inner-mind shifts when you do. Quantity is added to whatever you are focused on, not once but for the entire duration of your focus. Shift quickly, and less or no addition is made. You can change your focus and its emotional emphasis on anything. Do more of that, and faster. You can influence your company by focusing on what you are wanting—this is a literal analogy in this case. Your attention on the positive, or what you are wanting, and your willingness to shine a light on it, bring it up and make it a topic of conversation, make it your mood. Your company will register it as the thing to talk about—or they will be happier because you are (happy). You get what you want every single time, in other words.

Verbal work is what I call it. It is the verbal component of healing quantity. If you do not like new age mystic metaphysical terms, find a word that you like. You will not change the vibrational insertion. You are encouraged to substitute a word for one that you prefer, one that feels better to you. Always choose the path of happy or happier, no matter what. If you do not like the word "shift," use "flip-flop." If you do not like the "flip-flop," use "altered." If you do not like "altered," use "right side up." You get the idea.

Be sensitive to how you feel and always choose the word that feels good. Do not slow down your reading of this, or any book, because of it, of course, as you will lose comprehension. But there are certain spiritual-ish words that some of you might not be too keen about. If we were speaking one-on-one, I would choose a word for you that would resonate the best with your inner-mind. As a book, I give you choices. It is up to you to follow the guidance and discover word choices that feel good to you or find joy in the word that I present here. I say this to help you.

Chapter 2 ~ Influence

Verbal work is good for you to do. It is not a specific exercise, but it is good for you to keep in mind and do as often as it does come to mind. You do not know if your inner-mind is retrieving conversation and its content, or if your mind is in, that moment, quiet and receiving. Verbal work (verbal therapy is another phrase) is essential for increasing the frequency of and for accuracy in receiving from the nonphysical Guide of you.

Energy work is rotating energy of a different type in a direction that is good, on purpose. When you rotate energy in a positive direction, it works like centrifugal force and it picks up more strength. You may substitute speed. Anything that picks up speed continues without assistance for longer. What it does is very simple: it reverses that which it touches.

When thoughts coagulate and form a knot it is dense, negative energy that has drawn together or wound together. When large enough, it causes a problem for you. Touchpoint activation reverses the energy around the knot and begins to unravel it.

If you take a skein of yarn or two or three or five and you hold the ends together and you start looping them over and over, end over end, around and around, it becomes a ball. The ball was created by winding them together. Substitute that for harsh or critical thoughts (influence) of a harmful type. The strands of yarn are like your emotions, they bind together and form a knot.

Activating proper touchpoints will create positive circular motion around that "yarn" (energy block) ball—so much so that it will begin to loop itself backwards. You want that because that is how it gets smaller, and you feel better. We say "healed." Any block that gets smaller blocks less stuff. Simple as that.

Can you undo it all the way using touchpoint activation techniques? Yes, you can. It can be difficult for you to know which ones to do. Private guidance is always good to help you. The I AM Intensive or any of the retreat series are best should you want removal by us. Individual attention to the here and now, your active thoughts or those that have recently settled, can be taken care of on your own using Directed Energy techniques. If you do them often enough, you will begin to unravel energy blocks on your own.

What you want to be is untouchable by influence. Untouchable. That means you can be in a crowded room where people are arguing and your limitations, meaning stoppages in your Root chakra, are not affected. The combination of verbal work and energy work can help you get there.

End Chapter.

CHAPTER 3

Conveyance

*Your inner-mind cannot learn to interpret for us
on its own, nor because you ask it to.
It learns because we teach it,
and then it produces a thought, sensation,
aroma, or other conveyance to you.*

Chapter 3 ~ Conveyance

Session: 4, video #0704
November 18, 2021, 5:26 p.m.

Touchpoints are all over the body. The way you activate them is by hovering over one or more of them with another touchpoint. It is very simple work; not many of you do it. There are some cultures in the world that have good information on it. They do not have all of the information but there is some available to you. I want you to have our Knowing on this topic so it helps you. Misinformation does not equal healing, does not equal abilities progressing, and does not help you to manifest a life you are wanting.

Energy healing is something that people are starting to teach each other and that is good, but not all of it is accurate! I am being somewhat critical here to your teaching on this topic because we are wanting you to understand how to do it better. We want you to teach what we teach you and remain pure about it.

We want you to be a purist when it comes to following guidance. We want you to be a purist in life. How do you become a purist? Seek out Source guidance so we can teach you individually or in groups and keep handy your learning on these topics from us. How do you do that? Channeled works are one way, channeled workshops are another, channeled readings are another. We like those best. The guidance is deeper, richer, more specific to you and, best of all, we get to explain it in ways that work for your mind.

Simplistically speaking, are we going to tell you how to tie your shoes? We can, yes. It is an interesting example. If you have four children, all under the age of three, and two of them are showing signs of wanting to tie their own shoes, could that be something you ask us? Yes. Would we find it trivial? No. What is the best question for this topic? "I was planning on teaching like this…Is there any deviation that I should make for one or both children? My goal is that they learn it quickly, and without my accidentally belittling them."

That is all it is—accidental. When you do unfortunate things to your children and others, as well as to yourself, it is accidental—generally. It might seem trivial to you this type of question or the phrasing of it. It does not seem trivial to us. We say it is a beautiful coming together of human being and Guide.

How would we answer that question? Truthfully, not subjectively. We do not presume or assume, ever. We want all professional readers—ocular or otherwise—to be able to bring forth (receive) guidance that includes the details that this type of question is asking for. If you can do that accurately, you are what we refer to as "expert level." Now, full and open channelers can do that, always.

No matter what your ability is, we want you to decide what your specialty is. We want you to design your abilities on purpose. We want "difficult" topics or questions to not feel difficult to you. Simple yes/no accurate answers are delightful to us, but what if you want more than that? What if you want names? This is one of the more difficult topics for your minds unless you have made the conscious decision to ask that your Guide add it to your personal curriculum. Even so, you cannot know where the inaccuracies will crop up—and there are always inaccuracies. Ocular and intuited readings always have inaccurate components by a lot or a

Chapter 3 ~ Conveyance

little. The person does not decide a lot or little—the moment and the subject matter does.

You may have someone (a reader) who generally has very little ocular contribution to the reading. That means very little contribution from the Guide and so it is inaccurate from our standpoint. You have no way of knowing when the reader progresses and becomes more accurate. You do not know anything about their actual accuracy. We do. Always.

You are evaluating based on evidential information and that is not the best for you. You do not know if they are inaccurate and neither do they. Psychic tendencies are the biggest offender—bringing information to the mind by way of telepathy is what we mean here—which are not seen nor felt although validation might occur. It makes it rather difficult to know who to get a reading from.

You may find someone that suits you and, for the sake of book-writing, let's say that you have a perceived awareness that their accuracy is excellent. They have given (received and conveyed) predictions, and those predictions have come to be. They have given evidential information and that too can be accounted for. Unfortunately, the reason we say that you (nor they) cannot be certain of their accuracy is because human beings do go telepathic and draw information from you, in addition to us—a lot or a little, depending on the moment. The psychic preference is resolved with meditation; however, some evidential information, depending on the topic, never comes from us. The details of the death moment is one such topic.

The world at large has no clear understanding of ocular abilities, ocular activity, paranormal activity, ESP activity, channeled activity, talking with Loved Ones and Spirit People activity, or communing with the Guides activity. Misinformation is rampant because the world's population believes that you, that human beings, can teach yourself or be taught from another person to be able to have a conversation with us, to receive from us.

We make this a critical distinction. We have Teacher-student lessons. It is a curriculum that is given to the interior portion of your mind that can learn this topic and it is given in meditation. The only time we can do that is when you are in shallow to no-thought awareness. What is a shallow thought? No emotion, barely there, no time lapse noticed. Seeking no-thought meditation is most easily done by listening to a sound with eyes closed because even listening to a sound with the eyes open causes the inner-mind to take in too much data for a beginner.

We teach using words in the classroom, as well as in our books, to educate you. We teach silently in vibrational tones to train your mind in meditation. When you go to a class from a human, straightforward teacher, you are hearing the teacher speak. Your inner-mind has no idea how to do what you are asking it to do. It does not learn from a person how to interpret vibrational tones. They can educate you, but they cannot teach the inner-mind to receive from us. Your inner-mind cannot learn to interpret for us on its own, nor because you ask it to. It learns because we teach it, and then it produces a thought, sensation, aroma, or other conveyance to you.

The problem with human class instruction is that there is too much talking. We cannot supplement your lessons vibrationally because of it. What we would guide all of you to do if you wanted to hold a class—and any of you could do this—is quiet individual meditation time followed by a practice session. A development circle is what we recommend you organize.

It should be handled like this: "Let's all learn together, shall we? Ready. Close your eyes. I'll set the timer, let's begin." When the time is up, stand-up, stretch, sit back down, and play a game. "Let's all do Left-Right-Center," for example. "Everyone receive individually. Look to the right, receive something about that person, then look to the left and receive something from that person, and then finally look straight ahead and whoever is across from you, receive something about that person."

I want you to have your logbook every session. Enter the date and then itemize your practice session with an entry that identifies the game plus what you received, adding some detail about it for each of the activities. Get creative. Take turns leading or facilitating the circle. Whoever is leading, identify no more than three games for no more than twenty to twenty-five minutes after the group meditation session. The games can be anything. "Let's do colors. Let's do faces. Let's receive a memory. Let's receive an object that is important. Let's receive..."

Teach each other the difference between *retrieving* and *receiving*. When you verbally teach each other and reinforce it at every practice session, each of your inner-minds gets the lesson twice—once from you and again from us. We amplify it.

Do not retrieve, do receive. Receive, receive, receive,

receive. Ask each other, "What did you receive? How about you, what did you receive?" Being specific about using that word is excellent. "What did you get? Alright, everybody, what did you get?" Is not altogether bad, but it is not the very best. Think of it this way—if you were teaching grammar, would you reinforce poor grammar as you were speaking the instructions? I think not.

When you say, "What did you get?" There is no distinction between retrieving and receiving meaning, telepathic or ocular. "What did you receive?" is better if you teach the lesson first on the difference and then reinforce it in your spoken word. The inner-mind will learn faster to not retrieve. You would not think to say, "What did you retrieve?"—it is awkward-sounding but better for you. "What did you get," while more common, does not provide enough of a distinguisher for the mind. Using the words of the lesson—retrieve and receive is always best. Without this, it does not learn that one is better than the other and then does both—and your long-term accuracy suffers for it.

In practice sessions, you do not need to worry about accuracy. If you do not, you pressure yourselves less. Although it seems counterproductive it is exactly what the mind needs to become accurate, faster. The mind can become accurate. It is taught accuracy and your Guide is the Teacher. Your practice sessions themselves are not.

Do not judge the received image or thought, simply delight in it. "You received a rose. That's fun. Tell me more about it. What did it look like? How big was it? Was it three-dimensional? Did it move? What color was the background? Did it shimmer? Was there a color? Was it a sketch?" Ask

Chapter 3 ~ Conveyance

those questions each and every time. Draw more out from the person in their description. People have a way of limiting their description by stopping at the most obvious. It is good to verbalize in as much detail as you can however, and is why I recommend a facilitator, not a teacher!

Your logbook does not need all of that detail, but if you have the time, then do it. A list of ten things perhaps—"A rose, it was red with a green stem. It did have thorns. There was a black background. The petals were open. It was a full bloom rose. Single stem straight up and down. It appeared immediately. The edges of the petals were a lighter in color. It was large and very pretty."

The mind might have added nine of the ten and allowed one from us. We are not worried that the mind cannot be taught. So do not add worry where it does not belong. We do not error, so if we are not worried there is no reason for you to be. The mind can be taught accuracy and, over time, it will come about.

The common question is this: "Does that not reinforce the mind to be inaccurate if we don't seek accuracy?" No. As you recall, the instructions were to not judge right/wrong, received accurate, or received inaccurate. Simply identify and describe. It tells the mind what you noticed, and then your Guide gets to work on refining the details to be accurate. When you say, "The edges of the petals were lighter in color," the mind says, "Oh, she likes detail," then adds quantity to details. If you practice this way as your method and do it often, your mind will always add more detail than someone who does not practice in that way. Then your Guide has an opportunity to correct more details and you become more accurate on a variety of details. It is good to do this often.

During the meditation step, we will prepare the mind for the activity if the activity has been predetermined. It is always best to plan ahead for what the exercises will be. Simple is best so the newest present are not intimidated by the detail received by others. Break into groups and align yourselves by the level of detail typically received. Those who are able to identify a lot of detail go with the more detail group, not "more senior," not "more seasoned." Less detail group, moderate detail group, a lot of detail group is the structure that is my recommendation.

The next question often received is, "Does that not limit the detail received for those in attendance? Will they be unable to get more detail if they are not participating with the those in the greater detail group?" No. The mind feels less pressure so it will learn faster. You assume that groups are rigid. I want you to re-form them as participants progress.

If you, the human being, are wanting to be accurate, to have the "wow factor" with detail that can be understood by another person (validation), then your Guide will know it. If you are someone that wants to see faces, your Guide knows it. If you are someone that likes numbers and you want to be able to give numbers accurately, addresses, license plates, phone numbers, age—your Guide knows it.

Some things are more difficult than others. The way a question is presented can add more difficulty. If someone poses a question like this, "What happened to me on April 17, 2014?" and adds no other detail, the reader, the human being who is trying to receive, may spike in fear at being wrong and shut down rather than open up to that specific information.

Combining meditation, logbook entries, details to your entries, and grouping your development circles will give your Guide the best opportunity to teach your inner-mind what you are asking for. Remember this, we love you and we teach your mind what you are wanting.

What do you want to be known for? Design your ability—it is allowed! "So-and-so is great with addresses. You always know when he's connected, he gives you an address right off the bat." Or "Oh, I always go to her. I don't even have to ask my question, guidance starts pouring through."

That is fun, is it not? We are not training you in this book to be a practitioner of giving readings, but many of you will want to. Many of you are or will. We know that so we give you some examples. Development circles are good, divided by level of detail received is the best. If you are a human, straightforward facilitator, those kinds of circles can advance your learning and those in your circle sessions, without fail.

Channeled classes, if you can find them, are the very best if—and this is the important part—the class itself is trance channeled. I use the definition that is proper here—channeled is not receiving in general, it is allowing your Guide to speak out loud through you. There are some that channel your reading but not their classes. Do not go to them. We are the Teachers and we would like time with you in meditation but also in the classroom to give you our verbal instruction. You learn quicker and we resolve your questions as we go.

The mind's ability to receive depends on you and whether you have a quiet or quieted mind. Not just your demeanor—you can be a gentle person but have active thoughts. While you are having active thoughts, your quiet demeanor is not quiet. Quiet-minded means you easily remove thought, and when you do—"space out" is a good phrase that some of you will understand—we can offer the mind much in that moment, as long as your spacing out is not actually intense focus on decision-making, imagining something, creating something in the mind. If you have reached little to no thought then the mind has learned much in that moment. It will generally be moments—not an hour.

If you are having many bouts of lengthy, no-thought spacing out, do see a medical professional because there might be something they can do. I am talking about a minute or two or three—not hours of time lost, not blackouts. A moment of spacing out. Losing track of a few minutes while you stared off into space. The distinction is necessary.

When the mind learns in meditation, it learns easily. When the mind is not learning, it is either being given a lesson or it is not. If it is being given the lesson, it is learning. When it has learned, it knows it. There are no deviations. Once the mind has learned something we simply move on to the next lesson. There is an order that must be done, and each mind can vary greatly. That is why I say again and again, human beings are not the teachers. They cannot be, because they cannot retrain the ego mind/inner-mind. You can only educate each other on what you think you know.

End chapter.

CHAPTER 4

Imaginativeness

*Can you turn the tide on your financial wealth
by asking to see dollar bills?
Yes, yes you can.*

Chapter 4 ~ Imaginativeness

Session: 5, video #0705
November 18, 2021, 10:20 p.m.

Here we are. A couple more nights on the cruise. Time shifts back an hour around 3:00 a.m. The wind is blowing, boat is moving. Many of you would say, "The ship is rocking. I need Dramamine. I need to lie down." I say you need to get up, you need to have some fun, you need to dance and not know that anything was happening outdoors. It is when you reduce sensations or thoughts of them that you stop and pause, and accurately take in the current surroundings and make a decision on whether or not it is pleasing. The weather is different than earlier today but the cruise is still pleasing.

I want you to notice the words that I chose. I did not say, "The wind is blowing like mad outdoors. The ship was tossing and turning back and forth, waves crashing. We could barely walk straight, falling into the walls. It was altogether the worst night of the cruise." There is no storm outside, there are ocean waves but nothing tumultuous. The words that I chose were far different and describe the situation accurately.

It is an example of what I want you to do more often. When you exaggerate your circumstances you scare yourself as well as others. The words you think, the words you say, and the words you hear are the words that are taken in. Each of them add fear in general plus multiple specific events or situations. You do not know where fear will manifest. In this example, it might be boating or it might be staying up late. It is dark and it is currently nighttime on this cruise. The human being does not know which of the different fear quantities are growing. Do not worry about it, do not worry about which one. If it manifests, then do something about it. You can forward pave, you can preempt and you can postempt—all will help you. Worry adds quantity of worry so steer your thoughts from it.

Those of us in the nonphysical that are all present here in this conversation are the Beings that teach through people to guide you. We teach the same subject again and again. We also teach on things like how to live better, how to eat better, how to get along with each other better, how to love your world better, how to love your own personality better—in addition to how to know that we are Real. We do it in many different ways but generally we do follow the same set of rules.

"Follow Me" is a phrase that we always use through Carol. It simply means this; breathe in, breathe out slowly, wait for the out-breath to complete—and watch what happens. It is always in the out-breath completion that you receive from your Guide. It is a pause placement for the mind. In the pause, in the quiet, you hear us. You might receive a number or a word, but it will be verbal. It does not have meaning in the beginning. It is simply receiving something. There will always be receiving if done this way.

It is a fun game to play. If you are amongst friends of the same or similar skill level, take turns and let a conversation unfold—if your minds are quieted. If you are a beginner, do not try it. But if you have been doing your development circles, meditating daily, been keeping your logbook up-to-date, interested, and consistent in classes and/or circles, and each of you have been practicing the out breath "Follow Me"

Chapter 4 ~ Imaginativeness

game, then we can tell a story a little through each one of you when used in a group situation. It is fun. The receiving from each person will add to the last and become something understandable.

It is also an opportunity for you to understand that we are aware of who is in the room. It is a wonderful game for the inner-mind to learn trust. We are aware because we are there. We are talking amongst ourselves in a quiet way that you cannot hear. We are always present in the room with you. Who is the we? Your High Guide, any Spirit Helpers, your Divine Being—always. Loved Ones who you have asked to play a part in your life may also be there. That one depends on what you have asked them to do.

Another game is "Show Me." Pick any subject and watch how your Guide brings it to you. This one is an activity that occurs during your wakeful hours and not a development circle activity, because it is not an instant receiving game. When you request something specific and attempt the Show Me game your inner-mind is much too susceptible to your influence and can impair your ability to hear us. With Show Me, simply choose something simple: show me blue, show me yellow, show me white, show me threes, show me hearts, show me dollar bills.

Now there is a good one—I take that back, that is an excellent one—show me dollar bills! Play that one early, often, and consistently. Most of all, have fun with it. Not for the gaining of money, but for the softening of your resistance on money.

Who are you talking to when you ask to play this game? Your High Guide. They are the Being that answers everything that you ask for. When I first told Carol that the High Guide was basically God, she laughed until I explained it to her. They are your partner, your co-creator. They are the ones that answer everything you ask for. They are not the only ones involved, but they are the ones that form the plan along with your Divine Being.

They are responsible for implementing the plan on everything you ask for. "I'm hot, I need air conditioning" might be answered by cooling the core temperature of your body. You might not notice it, your inner-mind will. Or you might suddenly walk past a door that is open and feel a breeze. They are the ones that angle the breeze towards you or ask you without your knowing to walk past the door at that moment.

If your mind is quiet enough, intuition kicks in, meaning that quiet, non-verbal received thought or instruction. A received (or given) thought would be, "I think I'm going to go that direction" and then you walk past the door. You believe you had a thought, in other words. Instruction could be that you walk past that door, make the turn without thinking or deciding first, and then you feel a breeze that you were guided to. It happens this way all the time; it is called intuition and it is unheard, silent instruction for all of you.

When you ask to see dollar bills, you might see emojis, you might see coupons, you might hear people talking about things on sale, you might see a Lamborghini, you might find change everywhere. Money is money. What do you do if you see a penny when you are hoping for a dollar bill? You have lost the point of the game. Do not hope for anything. Pick the penny up or do not, but be happy to have found

Chapter 4 ~ Imaginativeness

the penny. I say pick the penny up, though, and keep it. It tells your mind you want all available money. That you are willing to take it in any increment for yourself. If you choose to spend the penny, great; that is a different game.

Can you turn the tide on your financial wealth by asking to see dollar bills? Yes, you can. You might want to add onto that particular Show Me. "I want to see dollar bills and I want them to accumulate in my wallet or my bank account." Create the AND. This is one of the pages that I want you to earmark. "Create the AND" means forcing yourself to add to your statement. It is good for you. Your mind will do what you are asking, rather than adding to it any of the negative thoughts that you have about money.

With this one, creating the AND is almost a requirement. If you have a belief, a limitation, that you are not worthy of abundance and you leave out a specific AND to your statement, you may get what the inner-mind has in it and not what you actually asked for. Such as, you may accumulate experiences where friends ask you to go on expensive vacations and you are not available or do not have the money for it. You are asking to see dollar bills. Spending money is seeing dollar bills. Conversations that include money is dollar bills to the inner-mind.

In the beginning, however, just have fun with it. "I want to see money, I want to notice money." Notice how many advertisements you start seeing. Not just the advertisement, but the dollar amount in them. Start paying attention to the larger amounts. "I want dollar bills to accumulate in my wallet." Better yet, "I like that I have plenty of money in my wallet." Plenty is a good word. It is not overused. It is better than "a lot" because plenty means that you can buy things and have some left over and you feel good about it. Practice creating the AND; it will save you some frustration.

It also is more accurate because it is more complete. When you want something, you want it for a reason, to use it or to enjoy it. Do not overlook the AND—and there is no need for there to be only one. That is the beauty of it. Have a string of them. It goes like this:

"I love money and I love that I see money everywhere. I love that it comes to me easily. I love money and how it accumulates. I love that I have plenty of it. I always have enough. Whenever I want to buy something, I always have enough. If I want to buy gifts for others, I always have enough. I have a knack for accumulating money. I love that about myself. I love me. I love my life. I love money. I love how easily money comes to me and I love how it accumulates. I love how much I have. I love that. I have plenty for everything that I am wanting." Now that will get you very far indeed.

Practice saying phrases like that out loud with inflection and add pauses. Pretend you are speaking to someone. It will make it seem more real. If your ears believe it, there is a very good chance that the ego mind will believe it as well. When it believes it, you start seeing it because it begins to add quantity to having it, rather than to envy for not having it.

If you make a statement that does not ring true, you are not fooling the inner-mind. Do not be hard on yourself. If you get tongue-tied do not stop; keep going briefly then wrap it up. It gets easier, and your life will be better for it. This may be used as often as you wish because it does not

Chapter 4 ~ Imaginativeness

overtax the mind. It is encouraged when you are sitting idle, rather than daydreaming randomly about things—typically, how bad they are, what could go wrong, how to get out of a jam, what your to-do list is, and how long it is.

Use your time more wisely. Imagination sessions such as these are much better than daydreaming every single time. Imagination Sessions. It is a different use of your time. It is time well spent. In the long run, you will not regret it because thoughts create your reality.

End chapter.

CHAPTER 5

Connection

*It is good for your mind to know how much
you enjoy and love anything and everything.
But for those of you that are wanting
to heal your bodies, heal your minds,
and heal your lives as well as communicate with us,
it is good for you to remind yourself
how much you adore having conversations
with your Guide.*

Chapter 5 ~ Connection

Session: 6, video #0707
November 19, 2021, 5:21 p.m.

We are still on the cruise ship headed to Fort Lauderdale. Las Olas Boulevard is where we are headed. It is area outside of Port Everglades, the cruise port in Fort Lauderdale. Carol's connection with us, her awakening, is not a twist of fate. It was life experience, and delayed life experience at that. She leaned into the Path to communicate with us through one reading and formed a belief in her that we were Real through another. The first story goes like this:

She was in the middle of a terrible breakup, and it had stayed with her far longer than we wanted it to. She was beginning her next phase of life; she did not know it. She was waiting for the breakup to come back together and unbreak like it had dozens of times before. When she bought her vacation, it was November 2018, perhaps October, approximately eighteen months into the breakup. She did not know us yet.

She was recovering slowly, but she was recovering. She had found meditation, but she was not recovering solely because of meditation, but because she found Esther Hicks and meditation. Carol knew of psychics; she was not unaware of metaphysical things. She had received readings on occasion during that time to calm her mind, to settle her emotions about what the future held. They were wrong in what they predicted. She tried various psychic, clairvoyant mediums trained in the art by people. Many of them made a living doing it.

Readings come in all forms: happy questions, sad

questions, need to know, would like to know, have to know, cannot handle another minute if I don't know questions. Carol felt some of those emotions, yet her questions were always the same. "What is happening with my love life?" She took notes. Her High Guide held her hand through it. How did they hold her hand? By steadying her emotions so she could hear not the words from the mediums, but her Guide, verbally.

True, she had a desire to know what the future had in store for her. It was also an indirect asking. All of you have direct and indirect asking, substitute questions. You ask for things without knowing it. During these few minutes at a time, when she was being soothed verbally from another human being (the psychic) who had connection with their own Guide, she was also soothed each and every time by her High Guide so that her mind would feel resonance with being able to do what they were doing.

It was a moment of connect the dots. It went something like this, "Hello, mind. Carol's going to have a reading, she is going to want to talk to someone who can speak to us. We want you to be able to do the same thing. It is what we are wanting for her. She wants to know what is coming up for her. We want you to be able to do what they do."

The readings that she received were highly inaccurate as well as highly incomplete. There were a few that panned out because some information got through. Clairvoyant readings always have inaccuracies. Sometimes a little, sometimes a lot. We like them anyway.

When you are focused on something, challenging subject or not, if it is part of your Intention (capital I) to have that

Chapter 5 ~ Connection

subject as part of your life experience; then, while you are focused on it, we breathe life to it vibrationally. We amplify it. When your physical focus is on the topic, we nab the opportunity to tell the mind to focus on us. In this case with Carol, we said, "Hey, this is a good subject. Pay attention to it, not the reading, the subject. Connecting with your Guide. Connecting with Source. Connecting with Infinite Intelligence."

Two people who gave readings to her stand out to her as friends although she has never met them. One gave her an idea, the other gave her our Knowing. The idea came first, it was a moment of highly accurate conveyance from us and proved useful. The idea came in a reading.

She had a moment of casual conversation with the medium and he described his start. He told her someone suggested to him that he visit a Spiritualist church. He was interested in connecting with Guides, understanding some of the experiences that he was having, and he began to go to their services.

The way he describes it, "It was like Spirit had slippers on until I began going to the Spiritualist church and then they had clogs on. I could hear them in ways I could not before." That planted the seed that was needed for Carol, that there are classes out there that she could take and learn how to do it. That thought had not occurred to her.

Here she is, with a mind who has been introduced to Esther Hicks. She has meditation happening. She has been drawn to psychic/mediumship readings. She happened to have a conversation with one who gave her a remarkable story—and she does not forget the story. It is funny how you sometimes think you do things but in fact it is your Guide asking you a question. "Dear one, how about do this? How about have this conversation? How about remember this?"

You have no idea how many ideas are received that way, how many decisions are received that way. Certainly not all of them, or we would not be having this conversation, but many indeed. I want you to have more guidance from us. It is guesswork the way that you go about it now, it is guesswork. Intuition, for all intents and purposes, is hit or miss unless there is something that we need to occur or to not occur.

Carol sat on the story that she had heard about going to a Spiritualist church and abilities suddenly magnifying for a number of months. It was intriguing to her. It took months of intuitional guidance for her to do one thing: find one. When she did it was not far away—imagine that—and she went. There are many things that you decide. When I say an idea, that means it is something new. When you have an idea and you cannot not do it, very often your Guide has had a hand in it.

Carol is Christian (Catholic) by birth and by choice as an adult. She stepped away from mass, went back again, stepped away, went back again. She still finds it comforting to have had religious upbringing. She finds it comforting, finds it good, better to have had it than not have it. It set some boundaries. She has that opinion because she has had life experience where she integrated herself with someone who did not have appreciation or love for church—or rules.

She found that person's children to be unruly, disrespectful, rude, obnoxious, mean-hearted, and deliberately cruel, with

Chapter 5 ~ Connection

no sense of right or wrong nor boundaries. Carol blames it on their upbringing. We agree to some extent. If you grow up in a free-for-all society you will activate the desire for it or to repel it. In this case, the children activated the desire for it. Carol could have activated the opposite in herself from her own upbringing, but she did not. So they were opposites, that is all.

There is no wrongdoing; however, there were too many intentional occasions of mental and emotional cruelty received by Carol. Am I sticking up for her? No. I am just telling the story. There was dislike on the part of Carol towards the children. She made some attempts to mask it, sometimes better than others. Generally, she had little interaction. When there was interaction, it was not friendliness that she received and that hurt her, not the children. They felt righteous.

How do you have an upbringing with no religion and feel righteous? Because they felt powerful. It was understood by them that they were hurting her as well as her relationship. That is the relationship that Carol was recovering from because, eventually, it shifted to a breakup. There was no final straw, there was an unraveling. Relationships unravel, and it is why we use this example for you. You can relate to it, many of you.

Energy blocks can unravel as well, but it has the opposite effect. It feels good, it feels better and better and better; you feel happier, more free, lighthearted; you have a better outlook. When you are cooped up inside and you go out, you feel better, a breath of fresh air—that sort of thing.

In this situation, Carol was remembering the story

of how that gentleman came upon stronger abilities and understood what he was able to do. He was given the idea that he could do it as a profession and chose to, simply by attending a Spiritualist church. Carol did not know what that meant (Spiritualist church). She pictured churches from her upbringing, a traditional church. In her mind, going to church was going to mass. She found out the services were far different.

Rather than a church, it is often a simple building with no religious artifacts but a sequence of events that are reminiscent of a church service. That was unsettling to Carol from the first time she went. Clearly, she followed through eventually on the idea of going because she too was having some quote, unquote "clairvoyant experiences." Her Guide was nurturing the idea of connecting with us intuitively.

Her Guide also led her to read up on the subject. She picked up a book, read it cover to cover on how to connect with your Spirit Guide. Generally, had no problems with the book. She has a critical eye but most of the book she simply agreed with. Her Guide helped her with that to make sure she would read the entire book.

We guide you to things and we guide you away from things. Carol was guided to a bookstore, guided to the aisle, and then guided to the book because it was an easy read. It was not unlike most, but it was laid out in a way that was simple yet had enough pages that it felt of substance.

Carol began with interest and she did the exercises. She sat at the same time each evening in the same chair each day, as the book suggested—only she also did her own thing. She "mysteriously" had a journal with her for the exercises

Chapter 5 ~ Connection

each and every time. That tells you something, or it ought to. She was expecting to get information. That expectation came from her Guide.

Most people sit down and forget their notebook, they just read. She did not. She mysteriously put the date and the hour as the header for each notetaking session. What she did different was she talked to us first—meaning "whoever was listening." She did not meditate first because her meditation, as instructed through Esther Hicks, was in the morning.

Carol would sit down in her red chair and would say, "I don't know who's listening, but I would like to practice. I want you to know that I might not be able to convey whatever you tell me, so please don't make it an important message for someone. This is just for practice. Is there anyone that would like to talk to me today?" It was always something like that. Very gentle, inquisitive, eager, expectant, shy. She received every time. She had images. She had faces. She had words, sometimes an entire phrase or two.

The strongest at that time were images. Carol would write them down with great detail. She would tell no one except her mother because the information that came was generally about family. Her mother went through the pieces of information one by one and told her what was accurate, what was not. There was some of both from day one. Some of that gives you an idea that there were several, sometimes many, things where the descriptions were validated. A lot of them. The ones that the mother did not know Carol mysteriously asked if she would relay the information to her aunt and double check. The mother did.

The aunt was able to validate a few more things. Notice

the plural. This was over the course of about a month. It was during this time that Carol was contemplating going to class. It was during this time that Carol had the conversation with the gentleman who mysteriously told her about his abilities growing from going to a Spiritualist church.

Then, finally, there was a day where she researched whether there were any nearby. She found one and was mysteriously very near to it. She had no desire to go to the service, but immediately looked up their events and found that they had a class. She decided to take it. Thursday evenings for an hour and a half; twenty dollars. That is what we all wanted. Not the class, not the church service. We wanted her to explore further the idea that was growing that she had a gift.

Ocular gift. She did; she does. She went to their classes, but not for long. She was excellent in comparison to the other students. There were others that also had connection and could describe things in similar detail, had been going for years or were professional readers who felt like joining class. Carol found herself equal to those after a month of self-study. Her excitement was far greater, though. Her notes were far more detailed. They were less nervous about receiving on demand.

She was good, and her attempts at receiving were validated. So much so that six weeks into weekly classes, that means six sessions, the teacher approached Carol and asked if she would participate in a public student demonstration. Carol said yes. Six weeks and she was asked to be on the platform to show an audience what classes can do for your abilities.

Chapter 5 ~ Connection

When it was Carol's turn she stepped to the front of the platform, held on to the podium as she was told to do, closed her eyes, breathed as she always does even still, and simply received image after image, after image, and then described them. Not all of them were validated. Carol did not like this. There was more pressure doing it this way on the platform, but she still received some validation. What she especially did not like was assistance from the teacher, who stepped in and contradicted what she received. This woman described Carol's receiving differently than Carol did. Neither were validated.

The air of authority from the teacher about knowing what Carol received better than she did perturbed Carol, albeit quietly. She did not show it but her enthusiasm for the class began to wane because of it. A month later, the same teacher asked Carol to participate in another public student demonstration. Carol said yes. Shortly afterwards, this teacher asked, "Would you mind coming to my Saturday class as well? I don't have very many students and I think it would be good for them to see how well you are progressing." So Carol did.

Not long after that, this teacher had a for-fee gallery reading scheduled not far from Carol's home. The teacher asked Carol if she would like to attend. Carol paid her forty dollars and went hoping to receive something—a message about her future, what was coming up for her, always silently hoping it had to do with her relationship mending. It did not.

Now, at this for-fee gallery reading that the teacher was having, there were ten people or so in attendance. Carol was one of them. Carol and the teacher sat side by side in a circle. It was not on purpose but convenient, because partway through the two-hour evening the teacher looked at Carol, not identifying her as a beginner, and said, "Are you receiving anything on that one? Because I'm not. Are you able to add anything?" Carol did.

It was not validated, but it was accurate. I have since told her that the person had forgotten, and that does happen and that her ocular sight was accurate. As every reader knows, sometimes connections are made after the reading. That is true because the person—the Spiritualist church calls them a "sitter," I just say the person paying for the reading—has strong focus, nervousness, or an emotional state causing memory to fade. Because of it, sometimes details are recalled later. Carol, however, wrote down what she received for several people because before the end of the night she was co-presenting. Some was validated.

She then began to pick and choose between Thursday or Saturday for class and decided to continue with Saturday. She liked the big open room of the Thursday class and she liked consistency. She had gotten to know the people a little bit, although not well (very shy she was and continues to be), but Saturdays fit her schedule better. The Saturday class had less people, but something different began to happen.

In meditation and throughout the day, Carol began to feel sensations. The air around her face, jaw, and neck felt different. She described it as a warmth around her or that the air was thicker, like a soft pressure around her neck. Her face, she said, had a rippling sensation, like a melting. She tried to find words to describe it. Her teacher did not understand what she was feeling. So, after describing it a

Chapter 5 ~ Connection

few times, Carol stopped mentioning it.

In these Saturday classes, Carol would sit on the floor, back against a cushion, comfortably seated. She began to make the connection that she was good, routine things began to occur. The sensation around her face and neck would come and go. She made the connection once that maybe it was a Loved One wanting to give her information and stuck with it. That was her first AGREEMENT. We used it from then on as her indicator, that is what I mean with Agreement.

She raised her hand to give a reading when she felt that pressure. Almost all of it was validated and is where the "nugget" that we still use in class and in readings came from. That is what she called it in those days. She would receive image after image after image and at the tail end she would hear an entire phrase. It was a message, the nugget of wisdom.

Now, this is two months into her classes. Once a week for ninety minutes. She understood male from female stepping forward, age, objects, body parts and more. She stayed in the focus the entire time. In the receiving mode. It was at that time a semi-trance state, although she knew it not. It is an altered state. She did not know those words either as the name or description of what she was feeling. She did know of three channels, all famous, none in person: Edgar Casey, Jane Roberts, and Esther Hicks.

She was fascinated with channeled material, trance channeled material. She looked it up in the Spiritualist catalog of classes and mentioned it to her teacher. "I think I want to go to England to take this class" and the teacher said, "Oh, that one's not for me. That one scares me." Carol

Manifestation of the True Self

laughed, "Really? It's the only one I want to take. The rest seem too easy."

You are guided in so many ways that you are oblivious to.

To recap, Carol followed through on taking class. Realized she was good, better than most, I say better than all. She was asked to participant in a student demonstration a month and a half in (no other new student was), then again a month later. Co-presented at a gallery reading on the spot without preparation. Her readings in class got better. It became an expectation from the other students that she would give a series of images and then "the nugget"—the message. It was how she wrapped up her readings.

The sensation around her face would recede and she would ignore class for a few moments and jot down what she recalled of the reading that she had just given to a classmate. None of the others did that. Carol felt driven to write it all down.

Then, suddenly, three months or so into classes, Carol no longer had the drive, the motivation to get to class. She did not want to arrive late; it was frowned upon. Her schedule suddenly became busier in the afternoon. Too many internal conflicts with the teacher's methods. What were the conflicts? Carol would give the description of an image, the person would think about what it was and try to make the connection. The teacher would jump in and say, "This is what I got. This is a better description. This is what you're seeing, Carol." And there it began, the unraveling.

Carol knew what she saw, knew that what the teacher was describing was not accurate. Certainly, it was not an accurate description of what Carol's mind was producing. A

Chapter 5 ~ Connection

notable example: Carol was sitting on the floor in Saturday class describing, in beautiful detail, the information that was coming through from someone's mother. Carol knew the gender, knew that the woman had passed somewhat recently, knew that there was a problem with the feet, knew there was also something with the eyes, but had not gotten the full sending.

What she saw was a stick, a long one pointing out and up first, and then down. Carol did not make the connection but was describing it. "It's a long stick like a cane. It looks something like a cane." So the spirit Mother changed the image to a hockey stick. Carol said, "Just a moment, it just changed to a hockey stick going back and forth."

This is where the teacher jumped in and said, "No, it is a cane. I see it as well." Carol was annoyed, number one, that the teacher jumped into the middle of her reading. She found that unprofessional. She did not like to be interrupted in that way. Highly annoyed in that moment, she did not shift out of the focus. Then the connection was made by Carol and the teacher was proven wrong.

Carol said, "Wait, it is not a hockey stick. Was your mother blind? Because I keep seeing feet and then eyes and then a pointer stick down like a hockey stick. It's going back and forth. Was there something wrong with your mother's eyes? Was she blind?"

The woman said, "Yes, my mother was going blind. She had terrible gout and it was affecting her eyesight." The images stopped there and the nugget came after.

Carol's annoyance shifted to what I would later call pestilence. It was pride surfacing. It was happy surfacing.

Her happy was restored through validation, because she had made the mental connection with the images that were being received, and also because she had been proven right and her teacher was again, incorrect. After one too many of those conflicts—where Carol was interrupted, corrected, and then her ocular image proved to be correct—and Carol suddenly stopped going to class.

Clearly, that is not the end of the story. Were we mad that she did not keep going to class? No. We helped to create the shift to not going. We simply wanted her mind introduced to some of the concepts of receiving and it was easier by way of a local class. So, we formed an energy instruction called "A Sending" and gave her an idea to get off the fence and take a class. We wanted her to see how good she was in comparison to others because she Intended (capital I) to use her abilities in this lifetime and she had not yet begun. Forty-seven, she was at that time.

Her Guide needed her to be introduced to some of the concepts, but she also needed a comparison. She was practicing on her own, speaking with her mother, hibernating in relationship recovery, had isolated a bit too much. She thought she was a beginner-beginner. That everyone received as much as she did. They do not. She had found joy in her surroundings, in her new home, in her new friends, in her new environment. Outwardly, she was recovering. Inwardly, not so much. Emotional balance was also needed.

YouTube proved to win the day, because that is how Carol "happened to" quote, unquote come across Esther Hicks and an Abraham video. She knew not of Abraham. She did not generally click on videos in her social media newsfeed. But

Chapter 5 ~ Connection

on this day, she did, mysteriously.

When an Intention is set the subconscious mind becomes susceptible on that subject. When that occurs, it is like owning a plant that you begin as a seed, versus a Chia Pet. You water both; one becomes a plant overnight and one does not but is in the becoming of it.

I am laughing to Carol at the moment, almost asking her permission to call her Chia as my new nickname for her. She was like a Chia Pet from receiving Source frequency beneath the words through the Abraham video.

For a moment, I speak to Carol: "Carol, you were like a Chia Pet. The voice of Abraham coming through Esther doused you with just enough for you to become a Chia Pet. It opened you up; the subconscious mind opened up to the Intention that had been there all along."

Back to the book. Carol's meditation was exactly as instructed. After she found the Abraham video and after she listened to it the first time, she was unable to not have Abraham on in the background every single day. All day, every day. She found one that she liked to fall asleep to, she found one that she liked to wake up to, and then found another and another and another. She simply found comfort in the advice given through Esther Hicks. Carol did not know about the undertone of Source frequency, but she did begin to learn that Esther was a channel. She did not know on that first day or the second or the third.

She bought their book *Ask and It is Given*, and read it cover to cover. She did not start at chapter one, she started at the preface. She read the story of how Esther's Unfoldment began. She found the story fascinating, and it was not forgotten but was set aside after she read it.

A month or more into these daily opportunities to be taught by Abraham through videos she began to feel better. The frequency of Source, if it is in the room, will bring comfort, will help you through any type of emotional distress. Just play it in the background. The Source frequency comes through a channel. Not to mention, the guidance was, of course, excellent for her. Not only that, Carol began to meditate in the way that Abraham instructed or used the Abraham guided meditation, and no others.

Carol likes routine. She likes programs. She jokes around and says she has just enough OCD to make life fun, not aggravating. But she does not generally stick to programs. Very rarely, she gets distracted, finds that it is not the best thing for her, and moves on to something else. She likes them but does not often complete them. She does not like that about herself. However, Abraham said one thing one time and it (mysteriously) stuck: "You do not have time to not meditate. Do it early in the day whenever possible."

After hearing that, she purchased the CDs and never missed a day of meditation, most of which were with Abraham and the healing tone of Source beneath the words. It is the very best way to calm the mind. The subconscious mind needs respite. Your bodies do as well. The body's way of receiving respite is different than the subconscious mind. It receives it in meditation—and more so when they are trance channeled as Abraham's are. The frequency of Source flows through the dimensions, through the human being, into the room. Electronics make no difference to us.

Four months into meditation, Carol's head began to move.

Chapter 5 ~ Connection

She delighted in it because she recalled the Unfoldment (awakening) of Esther. She had not expected it but the more she loved it, the more it grew. What was it—the head motion, the movement of the head swirling this way and that way, left and right, up and down, this circle that circle? Her Guide decided to give her one more mysterious thing, a phrase: "I don't know if this is the way my body receives energy or if it is information I am not yet translating."

Again and again and again they gave this phrase to her. She did not know where the phrase came from, but it came to her identically day after day. She could not get it off her mind—"Is it the way my body receives energy or is it information I am not yet translating?" Not yet translating, meaning perfect words, perfectly received.

She was, without knowing it, training her mind so that she would be able to translate. It never occurred to her how strange those words would be to someone else. To her, it was logical. It was the most natural phrase, the most natural thought. "Is it information I'm not yet translating?" It was a strange phrase, odd words perfectly received.

A number of months later, her High Guide simply did what was planned all along: communicated verbally. Now, the fun part of the story is that it began with her face. Her head turned left and words began in the air—letter by letter, word by word communication began. It was an extension of her ocular abilities. Her Guide saw it in her and it was determined that it would be brought it out.

She did not know that it was built-in then to channel. She does now. That initial conversation was not a scrambled word or phrase. It was intelligence. It was cursive writing.

It was dotted "I", crossed "t", capital and lowercase. It was a conversation. She wrote it all down, pages and pages, the very first day.

From there, they progressed her to automatic writing, followed by stretching the muscles of the mouth. Opening and closing. It was extremely simple with her. Her body had been attuned to Source for nearly a year. The undertone in the videos of Esther channeling Abraham did much for her abilities. As did her trust and enjoyment of the lessons. They would have come anyway, but it was smoother this way, not faster.

The stretching of the muscles, the asking of the mind by her High Guide to move the mouth, began as an open and close, open and close, and that is all. It took all of a minute or two and then her Guide was able to move her mouth in the shape of words. Conversation on the lips began, silent conversation as no voice was added. Carol called it "mouth-moving."

Less than two months after that, we posed a question to her as she was on the couch. The question "May we speak the words through you" were given to her using the mind's eye ability. She received it as a thought, not a voice.

As Carol laid on the couch, she simply had a thought, a sensation, a feeling, a knowing. "It feels like you want to say something," she said to us, thought it to us. She did that often, still does. Then she did what some do not. She allowed us to move the mouth and then spoke the word that was given to her mind at the same time. It was a knowing and a sensation. The knowing came first of what we were going to say and then we said it.

Chapter 5 ~ Connection

The only difference is, we added the voice. Hearing herself speak when she had not intended to struck her as odd for a moment, no more. Then we began to converse with her out loud. The way she tells it, "I went from mouth-moving to voice-giving." We like the phrase, we like the joy, we like the happiness, we like the love that was offered to us.

So many of you do that. It is good for your mind to know how much you enjoy and love anything and everything. But for those of you that are wanting to heal your bodies, heal your minds, and heal your lives as well as communicate with us, it is good for you to remind yourself how much you adore having conversations with your Guide.

That was it. A year of meditation and three months of a weekly class to invigorate her practice sessions gave her new ideas of things to do, and a lot of validation. It gave her the comparison that she was good, better than most. It caused her to feel ready to step into phase two: channeling. She did not know the Plan and that is sometimes good for you!

Why was it so easy for her? I describe that next—the tale of Carol's initial Unfoldment—as it is important for all of you. Number one, some things are built-in. Whether they are or not can make a difference, but if you do not follow through or you do not love what is built-in you might choose not to do it. You will feel loss and regret if you do not, because the subconscious mind will know that something Intended was not completed.

If there is a desire by that Greater Part of You—that Divine Being that decided to have this life and you are it and it says a specific Intention is a must-have—then it will come out. That is what happened with Carol. That is, essentially, the reason it was extremely easy.

Others have had similar experiences. Spontaneous channeling is incorrect—none of you spontaneously channels. You simply do not see it coming. We do, because we watch the mind. We train the mind. You sit in silence; we go to work. Carol was not expecting to become a trance channel, although she was extremely interested in how to do it. We influenced her using intuition. She did not hear us audibly and so she had no expectation, she had no demand on herself to do it. It was simple curiosity and no more. That made it even easier.

When the mantra was given to her—the statement, "Is this the way my body receives energy or is this information I am not yet translating"—she was also asked intuitively to repeat it. Some of the things that you do are being asked of you. It is always for a purpose. It is fun to find out what some of those things are, do not shy away from it. It will answer many questions about your own story, why you were driven to do this or that. Some of you make assumptions that are incorrect, we like to correct your thoughts on your life purposes. It is altogether one of the most fascinating types of readings that you can get.

When something comes easy or very easy it is often because it is built-in. Most of you are not unlike Carol and needing to be continuously guided to experiences that will get you where you need to be. That is the point of this chapter. You have Intentions that are all different. If there is something for you to do in this life, you will do it if it is a must-have. You can learn to do it even if it is not, but it will take longer. Trust yourselves. Trust your High Guide.

Chapter 5 ~ Connection

Do not give up on your ability to connect with us if your experience is different than someone like Carol's. She is not more special than you. Her Intentions were simply different.

Meditation is always the key to anything that you are wanting. Using Carol as an example, meditation combined with continuous healing from the frequency of Source allowed her High Guide to bring her to being able to experience an Intention that was a must-have. It was the key to unlock an ability that had been laid in place from the beginning.

Meditation is the key to learning. It is the key to undoing bad behavior. It is the key to fixing your lives. In meditation we provide a healing tone that soothes the subconscious mind. It prepares that part of the mind to learn something. We also guide you in mysterious ways.

We are Teachers and we teach the mind. We are Healers and we heal the mind. When do we do it? In meditation. We teach you how to make your way through life. We teach you to hear us, to communicate with us if/when you find an interest in it. We heal you by undoing the energy blocks within your bodies. Some of these are stoppages that prevent you from receiving or manifesting things that you have your heart set on.

When the mind is healed, your body follows. Your lives follow after that. Healing takes time. It is not a Band-Aid effect, it is done. When these stoppages are unraveled it means they are removed. A necklace that has a knot is a necklace with a knot. Same thing. When you patiently spend time loosening, moving, loosening, moving, loosening, and moving, eventually, the knot will no longer be there.

We want all of you to find your way to listening to channeled material. Reading books that are channeled and becoming perhaps a channel yourself (i.e., voice-giving is a particular ability. Many of you do use the word channeling synonymously with receiving in general. This is not the case. A healing tone is beneath the words always through a tranced channel. Pure healing is what the healing tone of channeled material will do for you. Combined with meditation, healing is occurring to the degree that can invigorate and change your lives.

Energy healing removes stoppages so you can live life easier with less weight, less baggage, less guilt, less fear, less anger—and less missed opportunities. The more you do it, the better you get, the more you do it, the better you get. Healing tones are a different type of receiving. It is not only available to everyone, but it is remarkable how much can be undone when you use it. We are undoing constantly to the extent that you will allow. Your thoughts make a difference, your emotions make a difference, your willingness to silently meditate makes a difference, channeled conversations make a difference.

I use this lengthy description of Carol's beginning to show you what combining these techniques will do for you. Her abilities came about not only because of a Birth Intention—many of you have them and do not find your way to them or do not find your way to allowing them to surface fully. A year of channeled videos as background noise, a channeled book or two, and consistent daily silent meditation—opened her to guidance. You call it synchronicities, I call it joyful expectation from us on what you get to experience!

Chapter 5 ~ Connection

Having an understanding that healing tone from the nonphysical dimension is something you can tap into, that it is available, that it is given, that it is useful, and that the healing is complete when done—is good for you. I want you to choose to integrate it into your lives. It is good that you do so.

End chapter.

CHAPTER 6

The Changed Person

*There are levels of dictation, levels of trance abilities.
The one you are or might experience is caused by
the belief systems that are in your Root chakra.
That is an absolute.*

Chapter 6 ~ The Changed Person

Session: 7, video #0708
November 19, 2021, 10:34 p.m.

We continue now and we are Jeshua, a group of us are teaching this chapter. Who are we? Beings that have learned all things about the worlds, and because of it we had a choice and we have all chosen to teach. We are Teachers of how to connect, communicate, and pass information through to the physical worlds.

Who are our students? You, when you are in the nonphysical! But also you, the human being, through this book. We like our job. We like communicating with Beings who are incarnating. It is necessary for us to do so. It makes your Higher Being grow, so to speak, when you learn how to use little-used or unused portions of your interior minds.

This configuration of us, the subcommittee of Teachers that was formed to bring forth certain topics through Carol, was given the name Jeshua by Carol's High Guide. There are many of us in this formed group. It was a testament to what would be taught through her – connecting with us, initially. She is knowing that we would explain the name sooner or later. She has been a channel in previous lifetimes and we have spoken through her before. Each time she finds her way to this ability it becomes easier to re-attune to us. Someone who can quiet their mind, still their thoughts enough to allow us to speak through them, is what we call a trance channel.

Many people have Intentions within to become a "changed person." We like that term for trance channels because it is an aspect of your Being that is dormant in the physical world that has awakened. We love the word awakened. It is accurate, to be sure. Serious students are not what we are referring to here, those that enjoy the subject more than most. We are referring to those of you that are undeniably drawn to it, that have experiences similar to those described in the last chapter—synchronicities and validation without much or any efforting. You may have an Intention that you do not know about. If so, your abilities will rise quicker, cleaner, more accurate. It is good to know that some things in life were meant to be easy.

If you are not a changed person, a trance channel, but do find that your ocular (substitute clairvoyant for those that have been trained in the ways of the world) abilities are validated often, do not stop your meditation nor your classroom or circle development. You can progress to changed and trance channel; it simply takes longer. Your abilities, the human mind's abilities, do not stop at image-maker and voice-maker, they progress to—to use Carol's words for it—voice-giving. We like to describe it as the ability to borrow your voice while you speak the words for us.

Carol is at ease during dictation now, in this lifetime. Her initial lives were different, although so was her attention on spiritual things in all of them. This lifetime is number four. Those of you that have found your way to this book and are changed people and found the ability to have come about extraordinarily easy, you too have lives to draw upon—better said, lives that have aided your development.

Your choice to follow the path of channeling is aiding your entire Being in the nonphysical. Do be at peace with your life, its changes, and who you were before the ability

Chapter 6 ~ The Changed Person

surfaced. It is a part of the whole, your life's story and yours in yours—allow your Guide or us to write your life's story in a way that benefits others. Let us give examples to many so that they too can find their way to an Intention to communicate with us. You do not know when you are the seed that is planted, which words, which stories, which examples will aid another.

There are levels of dictation, levels of trance abilities. The one you are or might experience is caused by the belief systems that are in your Root chakra. That is an absolute.

Your beliefs about trance channeling are multifaceted. If you are a deep channeler then the beliefs are causing your mind to shy away from the experience. The deeper you go, the less you remember when the trance moments are complete. Deeper still, the less you hear while it is occurring. The more energy work you do, chakra work to remove limited mindsets, the more you increase your potential for a lighter trance state. Why might you want this? We love this material for all of you!

Your mind learns by listening. When you hear us and feel the resonance of the undertone of Source at the same time, the material does not simply resonate—it is integrated. It alters your belief systems. What is a belief, but a knot, a coagulation of thoughts, that have lodged in your etheric body? All things that come about that you are not wanting stem from a Root ball.

Remove the knot, your lives get better. But you do not know who you will be when it does. We do. You will be easier-minded and have a softer outlook; less subjects will aggravate you; you will have a nicer disposition, and benefit

Manifestation of the True Self

of the doubt will be given to others without efforting.

Changed people—we love the title of this chapter because the title itself is influencing your inner-mind to want to—to WANT TO—let go of beliefs that are holding you from manifesting your truest self. It is a combination of techniques that will bring your bodies, your energy bodies and then your physical bodies, to what it was meant to be and who you were meant to become—a race of people that stay connected to your Guide Team. Your lives are changing simply from reading this material.

Absorb yourself in channeled works, any of you that consistently find yourselves saying meditation is difficult, that your mind wanders too much. Do this for one year. Make your homes and cars akin to a spa, where there is softly playing channeled material in the background—it does not need to be in the foreground capturing the attention of your aware self. The undertone is so easy for you to access, it is available freely in many cases. You have but to choose to use it.

This book came with a small fee, some videos are fee-less. Fee-less—there is awkwardness to the word for most of you. A year of background undertone in your life will make you enjoy, and perhaps find fondness, in using "fee-less" as a fun new phrase for free. We like fee-less and we also like for-profit, specifically for those who have aligned themselves to communicate with us for others and have businesses because of it or aspire to.

There is so much to teach you about trust, trust levels (substitute lack of it when we refer to beliefs), and connection with us. Your inner-minds are who we are talking to. Some

Chapter 6 ~ The Changed Person

of you will begin at this point in the series (Book 3 overall) to relax your minds on the uptightness within. Your thoughts will not wander exactly, but soften. It is part of the undoing process that is planned for those that read them in order, even more so if read back-to-back.

When/if you, while reading this chapter, find yourself noticing a small child sitting on your lap, a translucent child, or a person within or sitting next to you, you are receiving from us visually. Ocular visual sight internal (to the mind's eye) is occurring. It is a visual for you to use to extrapolate the meaning of inner-mind. There is an inner learner, one that was not available during your school sessions, one that slept through that entire portion of your life.

Once you began an interest in metaphysical things, it was then that this inner learner began to wake up and yawn only. If you have eagerness in the topic, investigating spiritual, even paranormal things, the inner learner is out of bed and brushing its teeth, wondering what it has on its chore list for the day.

Should you begin a path of learning about consciousness, who we really are, the way the worlds were created—non-religious, in-depth mindfulness studies—who Spirit People are, who Ascended Beings are and the like, your inner learner has decided for you that Conscious Life is important and put it at the top of the chore chart.

Dogear this chapter. It is excellent for you to read numerous times. The inner learner will eventually understand that IT is the one we are referring to. It does not know who you are. The veil, the barrier, the separation is that IT does not remember that it is inside the psyche of a human's mind in a physical sub-reality that you call Earth. It has not had that lightbulb go on, yet! But it will... That is our most exquisite description for you of law of attraction.

NOTE: For law of attraction enthusiasts, substitute the topic of spiritual awakening to any subject that interests people—relationships, behavioral changes, weight and body image, friendships, social engagements, work or work-life-balance, emotional setbacks and recovery from them, et cetera. The list is, quite truly, endless. When the inner learner wakes up and listens to us, you get stuff easier!

The inner learner is on a path of discovery and you are the OUTPUT of its thought pattern—only its thought pattern is telepathically received through your life's experience. What will you feed it? What will you gain from what you feed it? Feed it nonverbal love and interest in all things. Feed it nonverbal undertones so that it wakes up to the knowing that we are here, we are Real, and that we have cool answers for you! (Carol almost did not allow us to say "cool answers," and we are glad she did, for it is a good phrase that describes what we can bring to your life when you feed the inner learner the right nutrition.)

We use repetition as food for the inner learner and remind it throughout each book that we are the authors. It begins to pay attention to us because of it. Who are we? The Jeshua Collective of Teachers. Who is the woman we speak through, but a person who has quieted the mind in such a way that we are able to? She is the voice of The Jeshua Collective because this configuration of ascended Teachers was formed for her, for the teaching we plan to do through her.

If you remove the reverence most of you have for

Chapter 6 ~ The Changed Person

nonphysical Teachers you might see in your mind's eye a small child, hands folded, looking expectantly upward, and hearing or perceiving from the look on the child's face, "Please oh please let me speak through you, it is the most fun I can think of." That is your High Guide giving you an example of how we feel about you, and the opportunity to speak out loud through you. We do, by the way, have the same feelings about bringing anything to you that you have asked for, "Please oh please partner up with me, I have so many ideas that will excite you."

We continue, now, the conversation about trust.

Many people hear us. People receive from us intuitively. Nonverbal, silent, receiving, same thing. What you do not know is how often. It is always good to assume that you hear us. Be thankful for it and more will come. If you do not carry fear deeply, if you are not afraid often, no limiting beliefs that there are Beings of the light and Beings of the dark, your abilities will be easier for you to come by.

There is no way for you to be certain what your beliefs are. When a pebble is tossed into a pond, a ripple forms. The ripple is your life experience as you know it, on the surface. The pebble is underneath the surface. Should you investigate below the surface you would find hundreds, if not thousands, of pebbles—negative emotions. Which is the one that caused your recent experience? You do not know. You cannot possibly know, because it has settled into a position with others like it. We do know. We know what each individual pebble has created, manifested, done to you.

You know what schooling has taught you, what life experience has taught you—education, intellect, it is your learning. You have subconscious learning as well. Law of attraction is subconscious learning plus categorizing, labeling, and adding quantities based on what it has learned.

Retrieval is also a facet of the subconscious mind. That inner-mind, the inner learner, learns differently, at a different pace—sometimes more rapid, sometimes not at all.

If you are wanting to know what your beliefs are, look at your lives. Reason being, the ego mind, the subconscious mind, is a conductor. It bases its decisions on quantity. It is not, however, a thinker. It is almost automatic, almost. There is randomness at play, but the randomness is seen by us because we see the quantity, all of it.

When a change to the randomness is necessary, we intuit to you—a silent verbal offering to the mind to do something or to stop doing something. We have not abandoned you when you fall down, no matter how big that fall is. Your subconscious mind does not always hear us, does not always listen, does not always pay attention. When it does, your life begins to get better. Begins to.

The more you hear us, the smoother the path may be—or could be. Here we are talking about Carol, adding to the story now as an example of trust. Las Olas Boulevard, Fort Lauderdale, Florida, came about in a clairvoyant reading, with the second friend that we mentioned and someone that Carol had spoken to on several occasions. Interesting things were said to her by way of her Guide through this medium.

You never know for sure if the images in readings were accurate, meant for you, or if your imagination played a part in connecting the dots. Some things sound good, sound real. You may be able to make sense of it or piece it together. In retrospect, you might be able to look back on the reading and identify what was true or not true, what came to be and what did not.

True accuracy in the moment is good when you come across it. True accuracy is sometimes come upon later when we bring it to you. We piece it together for you with advanced knowing—do know this when some things in readings do not yet connect the dots for you.

When a name comes out of thin air and it is a name that you know, it might have come from the nonphysical dimension—a received thought. Or it might have been drawn from another individual psychically.

Psychic and telepathic are equal in the way we teach intuitive studies because they are. What the world does not know is that your language was formed long before you were born. The meaning and definitions already in the world on every topic that you have available to you. The meaning of going psychic, going telepathic they are synonyms. It means that you are drawing from the outer layer of the energy field of the person you are talking to. Generally, that is the most common way.

People use the term psychic (i.e., "I'm a psychic reader"), and it is altogether unfortunate for many reasons. Namely, it confuses people when words are used interchangeably. Psychic medium, intuitive psychic. We go through them one by one so that you have our terminology straight. All of us teach it the same way. The explanations we use here are to help you visualize and understand the definitions the way they are from us. And, at the same time, to teach your inner learner to not do psychic, but do mediumship, and to want more conversation from the nonphysical Beings available to it.

Know this first: people do not always use proper definitions. They use terms that sound good for advertising or terms that were taught to them. We do not want you to become a psychic. We do not want you to draw from another person, especially when you are supposed to be receiving from us. The term psychic/telepathic are interchangeable, we mean pulling from a person in the physical, not from a Being in the nonphysical. This is not useful. It is not harmful per say, but it is not useful.

A psychic medium would be someone (by use of the words) who receives information from the energy field of a person (psychic) and also receives from the nonphysical dimension (medium).

An intuitive psychic would be someone who has no idea how they know something—it may feel good, it may be foreboding—a good medium will not use intuition over abilities. Psychic, as we said, is pulling or drawing from another human being.

A medium straightforward would be someone who easily connects to Loved Ones, past lives, relatives. Individual lifetimes is what we mean here.

It is not understood what these terms are by the world. Basic advancement for you, and hopefully towards trusting our Knowing, means realizing that there is no easily identifiable term in your world's language for people whose inner-mind accesses, or prefers, Guides over individual lifetimes. Clairvoyant versus Medium does provide some clarification here but is not truly accurate. We use it, however,

Chapter 6 ~ The Changed Person

for the sake of your learning. A clairvoyant mind prefers tuning into Guides. A medium mind prefers tuning into Loved Ones.

Channeling would be someone who is in a quiet state—notice the word choice here. It is imperative for those of you aspiring to do what Carol and others like her do: cultivate a quiet state—not quiet mood, not joyful mood (not that your mood does not affect your ability to move into center (trance), but it is NOT a mood or pattern of thought). Channelers have an <u>ability</u> to quiet their mind to a degree that is useful for us (and for the world's population, otherwise we could not teach this way to you). It must be learned. It is advancement from clairvoyant and medium, it is advancement of your ocular abilities is the best explanation. We get to speak through you directly with this one! (smiling).

Interchange the words from there and you can come up with the proper definitions from their use. Now, again, human beings use terms that they LIKE to describe their business without regard, many times, for what the term does to the inner learner. Use psychic and say "I am" in front of it—it is what you will become. Every. Single. Time.

Clairvoyant medium is the best choice for all professionals. We do prefer Ocular-medium, but that is for your world to accept. If you shy away from the term, practice it before using it. Ask for help in accepting it fully before using it. Design your life with us. We love this book-writing to help each of you.

Automatic talking—channeling—however, is what we prefer for all of you. You GET TO, (emphasis is good here for the inner learner) have our conveyance of guidance.

Coaching is a good word choice too. Perhaps the best choice, because we do not force you to live lives according to our will. We coach you along your life Path and along your life goals (capital P and lowercase g, please, Carol).

Now for some examples:

If you want to know whether or not to buy a home and picturing the house in your mind again and again has been your favorite pastime for the last month and a half and you have a reading to confirm your decision, the reader might receive from you (go psychic) and say any number of things.

"I see a very large house and you. It feels to me as though it's yours." Scenario number one.

"I see question marks around you, but also a large home. It does appear that you're in it. Does that mean anything to you?" Scenario number two.

"No, I do not see you in a new home because I see distance between the you and the house, and to me, that means a no." Scenario number three.

On it goes, on and on it goes because people make assumptions in what they receive. They make agreements with their Guide, knowingly or unknowingly. They describe differently than we would like them to. They do not often ask for clarification or confirmation or validation from their Guide using Source-given Symbols (capital S).

So, what do you do? If you have been thinking about a house and you have a reading and the house is in the reading, is that validation that accuracy was involved? Many would say yes. We say no. The information could have come from you. There are thousands of people who offer their ability

Chapter 6 ~ The Changed Person

as their way of life. They do it often and they do become more accurate over time. But the human mind will still go psychic. That is not good. We do want all of you to ask your High Guide to shield you from being able to do that.

NOTE: Also, we love nuggets of wisdom (tips) for you as well . When you have a reading, ask that your High Guide shield YOU from allowing the draw from your energy field and then meditate for a day or two ahead of your reading. Your reader, no matter who they are, will receive—not retrieve—because of it. They may still go psychic, but not with your reading.

You cannot provide guidance, you cannot provide true messages from Spirit psychically. It is impossible, it is incorrect to say that you do. It is the main reason why readings are so often inaccurate. You talk yourself into the ability by how you describe your abilities, simple as that. Law of attraction is always at play.

If Person A has indecision and they have a reading to help resolve the problem, the reader might receive from us well enough to help you. Or they might retrieve from you and give you an answer which may or may not have matched that of your Guide. It is a problem.

Going telepathic is random. It is imprecise. It is reaching out, grabbing a thought, pulling it back from within the physical world. Now, a human being can learn to translate psychically-retrieved data. It is vibrational information and is why you do not realize when you are doing it. A thought is nothing but a vibration with intelligence weaved into it. The human mind can be taught to translate or interpret psychic draw accurately. But it is not helpful, and it is not guidance.

In addition, your mind does it randomly. You cannot count on it as a method of conversation with people either!

Another example:

We know the sky will be blue tomorrow, not today. Alright. Someone goes for a reading because they are wondering whether or not to spend time on the lake fishing tomorrow or today. The reader receives "the sky will be blue" or "blue sky." The reader may assume that this means that both days will be bright and sunny and gives you the okay for fishing on either day.

If they are a true ethical and professional reader, they will say exactly what they heard and no more. In this scenario, if the person acts upon the information and decides to go out on the boat today, they not only will get rained upon but also they may lose faith in the reader or perhaps readings overall.

There was some accuracy, but not enough. Our guidance was not conveyed. This occurs too often for you to believe in our ability to guide you. That is not what is supposed to happen in this world. You are meant to have verbal guidance, each and every one of you. But you have forgotten how to do it properly. We are the Teachers of it.

When a reader receives a partial conveyance, we can supplement using intuition to guide you. Had the person meditated ahead of time or had been doing so for a while, intuitional guidance would have been given for them to make a different decision and not get rained upon, AS WELL AS intuitional guidance to enjoy and have fun fishing in the rain if our guidance was not heard. We never stop guiding you, that is the point. Always.

Chapter 6 ~ The Changed Person

Now that may seem like a silly example, and it is. Readings generally involve more important questions. The more important the question, the more pressure on the person attempting to communicate with their Guide. It is casual, offhanded, like, "Hey, should I do this today or tomorrow?" versus "I'm considering investing in a home and I've narrowed it down to three, which is the best for me?" There is an enormous difference between those two questions. There is assumed pressure behind any financial investment questions.

When you are receiving, the mind knows pressure. You must practice under pressure without attempting fact-finding so that the mind does not take the easy route and go psychic, which it will do under pressure.

Knowing who to receive a reading from is no easy choice for any of you. Carol is no exception. She was very unsure of who to speak to, who to trust when she sought readings before her abilities surfaced. She based her own opinion on personality, feedback, trial and error, and narrowed it down to two.

She does not engage in psychic medium readings anymore. She will not have a reading from anyone who is not, as we would label them, a qualified trance channel and able to give the type of detailed (structured guidance) as we do through her. She understands the difference. Her trust level has gone down, not up, with traditional readings because of her channeled abilities. We like that because her trust level in us, in what we are able to bring forward with good training, has gone all the way up.

We agree with her and her opinion about clairvoyant-medium readings: they are not accurate enough. You cannot be sure when the information has come from the Guide and when it has not. Carol does not like trial and error, nor does anyone who is paying for a reading. So, what do you do? Pass on the idea of receiving guidance from the Beings who are watching over you because of potential inaccuracies? No. We want you to investigate and find a qualified channel, for though there are less of them they are more accurate.

The word channel or channeling is also used incorrectly, which is why research is needed. Many use it as a substitute for intuition, clairvoyance, or medium—for receiving in general. A channel, trance channel, is a different ability. It is advanced. It is "more-than" when used properly.

So how do you build trust in the professionals who offer their ability to communicate with a nonphysical dimension to you? How do you not lose faith that they are unable to get the details that you need to move forward in life with ease? Enjoy channeled material first—it is the best way to understand visually, intellectually, emotionally that we are speaking out loud through a person. Your minds recognize the undertone and help you with your belief in a channel. No undertone is felt by way of clairvoyant mediumship. The undertone is produced by way of what needs to be done to speak out loud through a person. That is a good step one.

But also, meditation helps with trust in general and all of you could use a douse of that. Your emotions are soothed in general in meditation, in addition to being taught something specific. Skepticism is not overlooked by your High Guide. You will not only gain trust or belief in us and our ability to guide you but, using law of attraction or heightened

Chapter 6 ~ The Changed Person

intuition, you will also draw or be guided to more accurate professionals of this work.

And then there is always the opportunity to meditate and study with a professional to learn trance channeling firsthand. You will feel the difference. Conveyance of information is different, more concrete, more of everything except details of death moments and things that may scare (do scare) the inner learner. We do not provide those details. We are also the ones who will teach a topic through you. Clairvoyant-mediums do not have that opportunity.

As the Teacher level, we speak through many. This particular configuration through Carol teaches The Essential Material—the Four Pillars of Learning to aid you in your development. Who we are and why you are having a physical life experience (Pillar 1), law of attraction (Pillar 2), how to self-heal using Directed Energy and other techniques (Pillar 3), and intuitive development (Pillar 4). Those four topics form the basis of our conversations. We weave them together in such a way that your inner mind learns who we are and then trusts that we are Real. That is the most important subject, always.

In addition, we also get to do more personalized things—talk to you through readings, private consultations, and groups of varying sizes because Carol likes to. She had Intended to allow us to write books in this lifetime and is doing that fully. Writing books was the Intention behind the ability to channel again. If she found it, books would be written. She also likes when we teach to groups of people through her, she likes the material and wants to do it broadly. She has fondness for us as well as trust, now.

Example three:

Trust began for Carol a long time ago, but every once in a while something occurs that improves it. Such is the case with Las Olas Boulevard and the second reading that was meaningful to her development.

Carol was asking questions of the gentleman who was giving her a reading. Out of the blue, not part of her questions, he simply said, "Next spring (2019) Las Olas Boulevard will be important to you. I do not know why but it's very clear. Spring of next year. Feels like a vacation and that it will be important for you to be there." Carol wrote it down and it was good that she did. She dated it—good that she did that too. She did not know what or where Las Olas Boulevard was, nor if she spelled it correctly.

A month or so went by over the winter months and she opened her email to find she had received one from Abraham-Hicks Publications. It was about the cruise she was intending to go on to hear Esther speak the words of Abraham. In that email was all of the information about when to arrive, how to arrive, where to arrive. All the way at the bottom, there was the address of the port in Fort Lauderdale, Pier 25. Her excitement lead her to mysteriously retrace her steps to the hotel she had booked for the night prior and it was there that validation finally came. The hotel was on Las Olas Boulevard.

Now, that is accuracy that we like—that you all can have! It is something that most people would say was undeniable—not only accurate, but excellent. The road name could not be mistaken as a guess, because who knows the street of a city in a country that they do not live in? This gentleman was

Chapter 6 ~ The Changed Person

from Scotland. Carol lived in Virginia at the time. She had purchased, but had not mentioned, a vacation leaving out of Fort Lauderdale and had no knowing of the street that her hotel was on. Surprise validation months later is truly fun.

We add our validation that he was accurate. The gentleman could have been accurate on anything in that reading—his mind chose to be on that item, which is why we say excellent. The validation of his reading pushed Carol's inner learner to believe instantly that we are Real. It understood during the reading that there was a connection. It, the subconscious mind, is vibrational by nature and can feel when there is a connection. It understood that there was. When Carol's exterior mind agreed with it (came upon validation), it—Carol's inner learner—was also validated and then duality of Trust occurred. The exterior and the interior parts of her found belief in us. The stamp of approval, more or less.

That type of dual validation is hard to come by. The inner mind is finicky and it was a True Coincidence. We liked it very much! He was drawing to him accuracy because his mind was in the receiving mode and it chose the road name. It was the piece of evidential information that created inner Trust for Carol.

If you know you had a blue teddy bear as a child and you have a reading, the person could identify a blue teddy bear. They could because it could come from you. That is psychic/telepathic retrieval. If your mother had a blue teddy bear and you never knew anything about it then it could not come from you. It must come from somewhere—that is the nonphysical connection.

That kind of validation is hard to come by. We talk at

length in this chapter so you understand why. When you do come upon it, savor it. It is rare and should not be. We are hoping to correct this in your world and in your inner-minds. But savor it as well because True Trust and Belief in Us could be the result. Believe that to be the case and it will be.

End chapter.

CHAPTER 7

Recognition

*We are not different than
your relatives who have passed,
from celebrities that have passed,
from gurus that have passed,
from iconic figures of history that have passed
— except for this: we have become Teachers
and no longer incarnate.*

Chapter 7 ~ Recognition

Session: 8, video #0710
Date: November 19, 2021, 11:26 p.m.

How does someone become accurate? How does someone build trust? How does someone design their abilities? How does someone come upon an idea? How does someone figure out what they want to wear? How does someone decide what to do, where to go, who to talk to?

How does someone—it is a great start to a chapter, not a great start to your day. Most of the time indecision plagues people. Too frequently, indecision is deciding not to decide, and the interior mind can do that to you. Do not let it.

When I say the subconscious mind, the interior mind, the ego mind, the egoic self, the inner-mind, I am referring to the aspect of you that collects and disseminates, categorizes, and labels, and adds quantity. It realizes which things you have the most of, along with what is currently on your mind. It begins to make connections based on the kind of things that it has in its filing cabinets.

If you have seen something, it knows it and you could get it—good, bad, perhaps indifferent. The way you cross your legs, the way you touch your face, the way you sit, the way you stand, how you feel about this, that, or the other thing. They are creations of the inner-mind based on influence that you have received.

I want to influence you differently, and I am. Every word, every page has a tone built-in beneath the words that you cannot hear. It is registered with the inner-mind as peace. The more you read this book, the more trusting Source to bring you peace goes up. Is peace happy? Is peace money in the bank? Is peace a new relationship? Is peace joyful experiences? Yes. They are all registered as happy and as "I want more of this." Those two things—happy and bring me more—are added to every area of your life, in general and on the specific subject moment by moment.

Your life gets better when your trust in us increases. Your trust increases when your mind is quiet. When your mind is quiet, it hears us—verbally, eventually.

It is the level at which we want all of your abilities to be. It is natural to have constant contact and communication with us. Some of you are just starting the learning journey of connection with us in a direct way. Reading a book of this type, channeled work, is by far the best place to begin. Your mind has not made errors yet. Of all the books on the shelves that you could choose on how to communicate with your Guide, you chose this one. Each of us in The Jeshua Collective, your Teachers, know each of you because your Guide communicated your finding of our book with us.

It is because of that Being that we know. We are watching you as you read the book. Not you, the external you so much, but your inner-mind. As it registers enjoyment, we speak to it and amplify joy so that it learns quietness better and faster. Vibrational teaching is occurring throughout your attention to the material. It is like doubling up. You enjoy, it enjoys, we amplify.

The mind does not mean to make a mess of your life, but it often does. Every time something goes wrong, it has a reason for it. There is always a reason. You attribute what goes wrong in your lives to us—it is a lesson I have to learn, if it was meant to be I would have it, if I was guided to it

Chapter 7 ~ Recognition

I must suffer through and endure it—that, my friends, is incorrect. We do not bring you hard times so that you can learn a lesson. We do like and enjoy that you find a silver lining on whatever your situation is. We do not like that you are teaching yourself that we could, would ever, bring you bad experiences.

It is altogether wrong. We cannot harm the mind. We cannot hurt your lives. We cannot be anything other than what we are—purity of love, purity of peace, purity, purity, purity. And there is no opposite of us. There are no dark Beings as we are the light. Those are fiction. You are human beings having a physical life experience, and we are the Beings that are tending to your needs.

I need to add this because too many of you read and take words the wrong way. When I say "we"—and do know we all love you so much and love that you have any amount of attention on us—do not teach yourself or others that we are different than you.

When I teach as "myself" I teach the Knowledge from the entity Being that I am. When I teach among The Jeshua Collective we one-voice the material by combining our thoughts. But we also use "we" to indicate nonphysical vibrational Beings in general. And here is where your learning needs improvement. When you leave this physical world, you are no different than us. You become a nonphysical vibrational Being. You have Knowledge at your fingertips that you do not yet have as a physical vibrational person.

We are Love Beings. We equals vibrational Beings. Vibrational Beings equals ALL Beings that are in the Spirit World. If you like that phrase better, use it. ALL people are part of an entity; an entity is synonymous with Higher Self, Evolved Consciousness.

That is the term we all need to use more often because you are beginning to use it. But you use it as if you are attempting to connect with something or someone different than yourselves. AS IF we are a different form of vibrational Being. When you try to connect with your relatives who have Transitioned you are—read slowly here—you are connecting to Evolved Consciousness. They are, they become, or they remember who they Really Are. Consciousness Beings.

We are not different than your relatives who have passed, from celebrities that have passed, from gurus that have passed, from iconic figures of history that have passed—except for this: we have become Teachers and no longer incarnate. We speak from our entity perspective, but we could and do bring out a personality that we have been. We have been people!

We are all the same type of consciousness. Let's be clear here about that: we are a type of consciousness that becomes a person. We are not the type that becomes plants, for example. That is what I mean by we are the same as you, you are the same as us.

We draw from our entire Soul Being and all of its lifetimes to teach you. We can also draw from a single incarnation (physical life) if and when we want to. Sometimes we draw from our own Teachers or they join us in our explanation.

We, in the most strict sense of the word, are consciousness. We are consciousness. You are consciousness. We are not currently having a physical life experience. You are. We are the Beings tending to your needs because you are there

Chapter 7 ~ Recognition

and we are here. If we were there and you were here, you would be tending to our needs! ☺ I have added that emoji and I do hope the editing process keeps it.

How do you prevent the mind, the subconscious part of it, from gathering and collecting things to wreak havoc in your life? Rereading explanations from us like the one I just gave you, but also energy work. The chakra system is vast and it is all connected. Circulating the energy in a healthy direction is what Directed Energy method does.

You eat lunch, you dirty a plate, you stick it in the dishwasher, you turn the dishwasher on and the plate comes out clean. Similarly, you wake up, you go about your day, you have an argument, you get angry about something, cry about something—your life has gotten dirty but there is no dishwasher to clean up your emotions. Directed Energy is the dishwasher. Later in the day, sit quietly and do Directed Energy techniques, and you will come out clean.

The quantity of anger, frustration, sadness that were added by your argument will be removed should you use Directed Energy methods and sequences. That is the unraveling needed to change your lives emotionally. When you do it often and add the verbal components—talking about your life as though it is happy, statements of appreciation, imagining your life abundant—you clean your emotional bonds even further. One is good, both is better.

Adding the third component, asking for our help, is best. When you ask us to amplify the touchpoints, we will. Learning Directed Energy method is a playful activity that is non-stressful. It is emotional healing that manifests as ease or easygoing, first, then more obvious signs such as mannerisms, behaviors, good luck or good timing. Then not-so-obvious signs as well, such as a bank account with more in it this month than last month, a gas gauge that stays fuller longer, the absence of arguing because it has shifted out of your experience.

We want you to begin with understanding that you have an energy body, then realize it has energy within it and the field of view within it is filthy. It is a slow and steady energy bath that will get your lives back on track. The sequences are many and unique forms can be given to you individually for specific situations, but there are general techniques for anyone. We call it maintenance.

The physical beginning is to create time and space in your life for it. Start recognizing that you have hands and feet and get curious how they can be used. They are your starting point, they are the ending point, they are your touchpoint activators. We teach you to begin at your Crown chakra and work your way down when doing a full sequence or anywhere you like if you simply want to apply something.

Sequences are hands-on techniques that are easy. They are structured, but they are easy. You may do them sitting up, laying down in a bathtub, lying in the sun, from a beanbag chair on the floor, in bed. It matters not as long as you are not actively talking, watching television, or engaging in some kind of activity.

It is a meditation-like scenario that you are after to receive the full effect. Soft music is okay as long as it is not harmful music. A peaceful, gentle sound, something that is pleasing to you, is good. I do not want you to become bored with it because I want it to become a practice. Create space in

Chapter 7 ~ Recognition

your day. Create space in your home, if you like, make it a pretty area that is comfortable. Some of you have meditation rooms or mats. Do that if you like. Make it fun, make it a practice, just do it.

Your hands are powerful. When used properly, they can activate all of the touchpoints in the body, one by one. When touchpoints are activated, it is like turning on a fan and pointing it in the right direction. It pushes energy forward. Whatever is in its path, shifts. The amount of shifting depends on how long you stay in the position of the touchpoint being activated. It is very simple and, yes, it can heal your lives.

Beliefs, limitations, mannerisms, physical problems, emotional problems, money problems, relationship problems, boredom problems, systemic problems of every variety can be healed.

They must be slowed down, then reversed, and then pushed in the proper direction. But it can be done and no medication is required!

End chapter.

CHAPTER 8

Purification

*You have purified past lives,
not past lives by themselves as they were.
There is such an enormous difference.
Your comprehension of All That Is does depend
on your understanding those very words.*

Chapter 8 ~ Purification

Session: 9, video #0711
Date: November 20, 2021, 9:34 a.m.

You are, some of you, beginning to have the light bulb go on. Law of attraction, plus energy work is how you get stuff. Clean your thoughts, clean your energy body, and life gets back to what it should be. We all call it "normalizing."

At this point, I have laid the foundation of how the mind works, how the inner-attractor is really you, how law of attraction is you as an individual, instructed you on retrieval versus receiving, who we are and why you ought to be connecting with us directly and often, why psychic is a word to not use, and introduced the idea of energy baths. I have planted a lot of seeds in your inner-minds. I am enjoying this activity!

Every single lifetime you carry forward nothing except what that Greater Part of You is wanting you to carry forward. So stop blaming all your problems on a past life showing up. That is not the case.

If a past life is an aspect of you, it is not the foundation of your personality. It would be an aspect that is useful because You, your nonphysical Being, wanted it to be. If life experience has brought you something that you do not enjoy, that is not a past life messing with you. It is not a shadow figure haunting you. It is not a dark entity looming over you. It is not bad at all.

Everything, if you have understood the Transition (capital T), is purified upon completion of it. The purification process removes all ill will, all emotional discord, and your attachment to it.

An example: forgetfulness—emotional discord. You no longer believe after your Transition that you were forgetful. You simply see your life's story, all thought patterns, emotional patterns, attractor patterns and how the accumulation occurred. How accumulation manifested a personality trait that remembered things less often than others.

If there were no comparison happening during your life's experience, you would have been happy with not remembering things as much. Forgetfulness would not have registered as the word to use for the personality trait nor something that was not wanted. Your word choice makes a difference. The comparison might have been to your former self or a different person, it matters not who.

If you need a moment to reread that paragraph, do so. It is important that you understand who we are—trust is at stake here and we are wanting you to trust us. In the purification process, all emotional patterns are removed, all unhealthy limitations are removed for all of you—as it was for us when it was us—so that you can see clearly and continue your Being's ascension project (20/20 sight, allegorically, after the Transition is complete).

We do not carry our personality on our shoulders like a cloak. We carry aspects of our Being within us, as do you. The aspects are purified. What is an aspect? In the physical, it is a personality trait, who you present yourself as to the world at large, who you think yourself to be. In the nonphysical an aspect is the very same thing but without its detrimental secondary descriptor, the emotional layer added to it. This emotional barrier is what we are normalizing, removing,

Chapter 8 ~ Purification

and reducing in many cases.

Who you Are is who you have become by way of the Transition, not by way of life experience. It is like a child who goes outdoors to play. They are having a wonderful time playing baseball, perhaps, and sliding to first base or second or third. It is joy plus dirt. Sometimes a lot of dirt. Sometimes more dirt than anything else. When the child comes home it is a dirty happy kid, or a dirty unhappy kid—both are experienced from time to time. How much of one versus the other is also life experience.

When that child is called home for dinner and rushes in, baseball glove and ball in hand, and his mother sees that as well as his filthy hands, she tells him to shower (Indulge me here a little bit for I am adding much of what is not occurring but for analogy's sake I must) completely and remove all trace of dirt. She says that he will know when his shower is complete because he will feel no trace of dirt on his skin, see no dirt under his fingernails, no grit in his teeth, and, magically, no scrapes or cuts from the game will remain. He will be cloaked in pure joy at having had an amazing day, an amazing game, and looking forward to an amazing dinner with his amazing family. He is purified. He is clean. He has completed the Transition (to tie it all together) or, in energetic terms, completed the final attunement.

This is, analogy specificness excluded, exactly how it is. You are sent to your room to shower and bathe, and you come out clean as a whistle with a disposition to match! Minor difference for those who are particular, the final attunement or shower (I truly do love metaphors) is conducted to you and for you. You are like a prince (not a prisoner) who gets bathed and feels joyful having it done.

This is Truth (capital T) for all persons, all people, all boys and girls, men and women, all truck drivers, military members, nurses, captains, stay-at-home mothers, kids, and grandparents. It matters not who you are, what you have done, what life caused you to do or what life choices occurred. Your Transition, your spiritual bath, your princely shower is COMPLETED—no exceptions, not ever.

Each and every one of you comes into your full Being bathed and robed in glory. Purified. Purity of Love. Purity of Life. Purity of Soul Essence activity of the physical world. Purity of meat and potatoes kind of living. Purity. Purity. Purity. It is who you are, whoever you are, so forget the past and look forward to that! But do energy baths as a physical person as well and your princely shower will take less time and fewer Guides to help you.

Life experience adds color to your Being. Energy showers are good for you. All unhealthy patterns of thought are removed. You no longer see someone as bad or ugly or fat or mean or nasty or cruel or a brat. You see them as a person who is living life and doing the same thing as you—creating patterns. Their pattern may have been far different than yours, but it is just a pattern.

The pattern of who they are in this lifetime, if it is unhealthy, unnatural, not born of love, it will be removed. Simple. Purified. You have purified past lives, not past lives by themselves as they were. There is such an enormous difference. Your comprehension of All That Is does depend on your understanding those very words. If you understood nothing else from any book that was ever written, those

Chapter 8 ~ Purification

words are the most important for you.

Your lives are an accumulation of pure experience, you were loved into being and you are love at the core of who you are. Everything about your Being in the nonphysical exudes love—your perception included. All is purified. Every lifetime that you have ever had, purity describes all of them, no matter who you were.

Fear not. Live your lives. Guilt not. Live your lives. Harm not. Live your lives. Belittle not. Live your lives. When you do, you also savor life experience and create the opportunity for others to do the same. If they do, great; if they do not, okay.

If you feel good day after day after day, simple meditation and simple energy work is still required. Life experience adds quantity to your inner-attractor no matter what. Limiting the accumulation prevents unhealthy beliefs from forming. These beliefs shape your life. Energy work reduces the accumulation and, in time, trains the inner-mind to add quantity slower and on less items.

It is the quantities of negative living that are purified. The Transition removes what is remaining. Energy work in all its forms reduces and removes at a rate that you do it, and that, my dear ones, is the why for it—it reshapes your lives for the better. Energy work enhances positive quantities and quiets the mind. When the mind is quiet, it hears us.

Law of attraction does bring you some of both—things you are not wanting and things that you are wanting. However, law of attraction, the inner-attractor, the creating that occurs in this world, is random, not specific, in what it brings to you by way of quantities and subjects. Energy work allows us to turn random into specific. We do not become your law of attraction, but your attractor begins to hear us and listens to the Plans that we have for you.

There are more tentacles to negative emotions than you are aware of. How many ways can you define anger? How many synonyms can you find that define anger? They are almost endless. One word could be exchanged for thirty others, each of those thirty more, each of those thirty more, each of those thirty more. The emotional scale is variety in action.

The inner-attractor activates quantity. Several at a time, constantly. What you draw to you is what you think about, however, what you think about are those things that are prevalent. If you like what you think about, do a lot more of it, but get specific. If you do not like what you are thinking about, change it up immediately because every moment that you do not, accumulation occurs. That is the reason why it is hard to get off the subject.

We acknowledge it. It is hard to get off the subject, but not impossible. There are tricks—some of them intentional living, intentional thinking, and intentional imagination sessions. We love sticky notes, for instance, for positive ideas. They are transferable. Leave them in places that are easy to see, and they will remind you of easy, go-to topics that transform you thought patterns. They are your U-turn, your persuasive distraction, decided upon by you. They help you form a positive habit, that of verbal therapy.

Affirmation decks, books, or journals where you have written nothing but happy notes to yourself—read one or two or three or write in them daily. Go outside, look up,

Chapter 8 ~ Purification

and be thankful for your life. Those are ways of activating or pursuing positive thought that are in addition to, or an extension of, Directing Energy within.

Directed Energy is the process by which interior energy of the etheric is motion-activated by way of nonphysical vortex points. These activation points within your body are what we call touchpoints, and they aid positive thought. It is a boosting effect. Some of you will not enjoy it, find it boring, and be unsure if it is working. If so, stop doing it. Let your life unfold. Energy work is a silent helper that heals.

You put a Band-Aid on a cut, you shower, you live your life, you forget about it. You remove the Band-Aid and—voila!—it is Healed. How does your body know that you need healing? How does the body know to activate healing memory receptors? Cellular memory of what is correct. That where it is, is not where it should be. Cellular memory, cellular consciousness, begins to recreate the healthy (normalized) position so that it may continue its life purpose.

Be like your cells when you are feeling less-than. Bring forward thought memory that is healthy. Tend to your emotional wounds using positive thought. Normalize that which is occurring to you, emotionally. Directed Energy is a cooperative component for inner healing of the etheric energy components. It is available to you. It is what we teach next.

End chapter.

CHAPTER 9

Free Flow of Ideas

*That is the part that so many of you are missing.
Law of attraction is not us.
We do not give you some of both—
"I want it, I cannot have it." We cannot.
We have nothing in us except purity of positivity.*

Chapter 9 ~ Free Flow of Ideas

Session: 10, video #0712
Date: November 20, 2021, 11:37 a.m.

Today is the last day of the cruise. It is Saturday, November 20, 2021, and it is 11:37 a.m. I looked down at the clock because Carol's mind has in it that it must be precise, and she has not yet learned to allow me every time to say the correct numbers without seeing them first. She has this push and pull on the inside. "I want this, I don't know if I can have it." She has also figured out that there are some things she cannot do—yet.

She likes that word—yet. So do I. I do mind that she is aware of the yet because it holds her apart from what it is that I want to give her—in this case, precise clock time. I will say, "Late morning"; "Early afternoon"; "Eleven-something" and be correct. She wants precise accuracy. She has asked me to teach her mind to allow me to say specific numbers, and that includes time.

Now, I am able to give her preciseness in many ways on this topic, on this asking. She is accurate with allowing timing, timeframes, but we have an agreement to use a number wheel to verify dates and clock time, for example. Her mind is aware of this limitation. She does not like it.

Precise accuracy is available to all of you. You have to settle your mind down. You have to remove doubt on the inside. I like to say it is the internal you that holds you apart. Some of you get down on yourselves, much too self-critical, but there is understanding coming. I want you to know that we have not abandoned you in your quest to manifest. I want you to understand that you *are* manifesting. The better thing for you to say is, "I manifested what I wanted and it was easy, it came quickly to me, it always does."

That is general happy, general hopeful expectation. The inner-mind lays that generality across all quantities of happy on every variation, every subject. Generality is applied to all topics in your life's experience. There is no better phrase for you to say. On occasion, get a specific "I always have" and fill in the blank—again, on occasion only. All other times, use the general statement, and it will allow you to re-create your reality.

Use this technique. It is verbal therapy for the inner-mind so that it softens itself (its thoughts that manifest or do not manifest your wants and needs)—in general. That includes feeling uptight or upside-down thinking. When upside-down thinking is correct, then getting specific—and feeling good the whole time—is easier. There is a process to it and most of you start a few steps further than the actual starting place for you, individually.

You are creators at the core of who you are; we all are. That is what the subconscious mind is doing with all the filing and retrieving. It is creating for you. The energy of Source flows through your etheric field, your energy field. It is the invisible part of you. It is there, although you do not have awareness or education on it. Law of attraction is there as well. It is the attractor. It is your own attractor.

That is the part that so many of you are missing. Law of attraction is not us. We do not give you some of both—"I want it, I cannot have it." We cannot. We have nothing in us except purity of positivity, purity of positivity. We are love carnate Beings.

Chapter 9 ~ Free Flow of Ideas

Whatever you think about you do get, one way or the other. If you think about happy, you will bump into more happy people, but you might literally bump into them hitting shoulder to shoulder or bumper to bumper on your car because you think too much about things that have gone wrong. You get some of both. Your bumper-to-bumper incident ends up as a simple exchange of insurance information or a fistfight, depending on where you are in the spectrum of, or quantity of, both happy and unhappy. Always tip the scales to happy. It is the reason for both meditation and verbal happy projection of life.

Meditation is the key to the slow and steady disintegration of the dense vibration that causes your inner-mind to retrieve that which you are not wanting. It adds its own subject to your emotional setpoint. When I say you are a different person every second, you are. If your eyes are open and you are staring out the window, you are taking in a different view second by second by second. If you are looking at a tree and the tree is lovely, you are adding quantity to trees to lovely to green things, to windy days, perhaps to outdoors, to staying inside.

Therein lies the duality problem, because there might be a preference to be indoors if it is chilly or outdoors if it is sunny, hence the quantity addition to both indoors and outdoors. That, my friends, is conflict within because you cannot have both at the exact same moment. Quantity of have and have not is present. It cannot be otherwise unless you teach yourself some pretty basic concepts—be happy all the time, at least in your words, and emotions might follow.

Even in the moment of appreciation, your mind is adding

quantity to both. Always tip the balance or believe that you are. If you say, "I am working on tipping the balance" you are not yet at the peak. If you say, "I tipped the balance in my favor," you are over the peak. Enough said.

Project where you are wanting to be. Look back and appreciate being there and talk about it as though you have it, it was easy to come by, and that manifesting easily is something you do all the time on everything. We call it the statement of appreciation. It is looking at your situation in a rearview mirror. Only you have to project yourself into the future to use its rearview, not the one you currently have. Do not use future tense in this, past tense is what you are after.

If you do, more things will reach the peak and continue in your favor. Using the word "sometimes" in your appreciation statement might feel more real—using "always," not so much, but is better for your ability to create. Find the right balance of words, emotional conveyance, and even body language. It will cause you to feel as though you are having a conversation about your perfect situation.

That is where inflection and tone create a casual pretend conversation with another. Only using your half of the conversation is a wise technique with this. It adds instant memory recall and that, my friends, is a belief in the making. Once you have convinced YOUR mind that you have something, it must bring it to you. When you get the hang of it, you should use it often.

Example one: You are wanting to go on vacation and you have not picked a place, you are unsure if you will have the money or the time but you long to do what others do—vacation and spend money as if it were nothing. I want

Chapter 9 ~ Free Flow of Ideas

you to see vacation, not as a bill, but as an opportunity to see the world and forget about the money. How do you forget about the money if you are currently having a hard time covering your bills, yet you want to go on vacation like everyone else?

Know this: not everyone goes on vacation. Some people go on vacation, some people talk a lot about their vacation and then have debt for the rest of the year that they do not talk about. It becomes habit and it is their way of vacationing. Do not envy others, because you do not know their situation nor their bank accounts. Simply create what you are wanting differently.

Practicing the statement of appreciation might go like this—remember here, this statement is used before you go on vacation, it is a projection technique to train the innermind to bring it to you. You are creating, in a real way, that which you are WANTING TO EXPERIENCE. Talk about what you WANT ONLY.

"I love vacation. Every time I go, it is so relaxing. I love going in the spring and the fall. My summer vacations are so lovely, and my winter vacations are so much fun. I love where I go. I love how often I go. I love that it was this place and this place. I always have a good time selecting where to go next. Ideas come easy to me. Vacations come easy to me. I always make friends wherever I go and it is easy to stay in touch with them. We always have conversations back and forth. I have so many friends from all over the world. We get together on this island or that mountaintop. I've seen the world and it's been a delightful life. I love my life. I love vacations."

Money was nowhere in that entire imagination moment. If you are very uptight about money, leave that subject out altogether. You will naturally add it in and your free-flow, extended statements of appreciation, at some point will sound something like this:

"I love vacation. I love that I always go on vacation, I love that it's easy to go on vacation. There's always time and there is always money and both always come easily to me. There's always friends, there's always places to go, and I always have the time to go. I think vacationing is what I love the most about every season. I'm always planning my next vacation. The location is always the perfect place for me, and it's easy to know where to go. It just feels good. Life feels good. Money feels good. Friends feel good. I enjoy having money and spending money always feels fun. There's always enough. There's always plenty. I always have more than enough. There's always more. Money is always coming in. I always have more money than I could ever spend. I just have this easy way of drawing money to me and I love spending it on vacations."

Sometimes can be all the time if you free flow this way. The pathway to it—your words—matter. The emotional tone that you add to the words matters. If you find that you are doing this imagination moment and it feels really good then leave it there, say no more. Later in the day or a week later, when you think about vacation, and you get that rumbly feeling in your chest—the sign of worry—stop in that moment and do something else. Distract yourself. If that does not work or if it feels good to you to do so, free flow again, adding verbal joy about vacations.

Chapter 9 ~ Free Flow of Ideas

Recover and then, recover and then. It is a string of thoughts that go in order emotionally. Leave your emotions in a better place and the minds finds happy easier. Over time, the mind finds happy plus the subject—vacation and happy together, money and happy together. When the mind starts to combine a subject with emotion, things start coming to you easier. Keep it going, love on it, and it starts to come faster. That is where you all want to be. Words matter greatly in this physicality.

Boosting the words with energy work turns the tide. Some of you wonder why you do not get what you are wanting. You think hard, you do the work, you journal, you stay happy on the subject or in general. You have vision boards. You design, you create—and you wait. You design, you create—and you wait and it does not seem to come or not enough of it to make it feel satisfying. There is a missing piece to your understanding—how the Root chakra affects your ability to manifest on purpose.

CHAPTER 10

Cleansing the Root Chakra

*You manifest your life,
but there are ways for you to do a better job of it.
What you think about you get more of,
what you love upon you get faster.*

Chapter 10 ~ Cleansing the Root Chakra

Session: 10, video #0712
Date: November 20, 2021, 12:00 p.m.

If you could see what we see, the Root is clogged. It is not a crystal-clear, invisible bubble around you, this energy field. It is cloudy, it is quicksand, it is muddy—it is clogged. Energy work, the activation of touchpoints, is like turning a washing machine on for your energy field. It cleanses it.

When the energy field is cleaner, your limitations are less pronounced in your lives. You do create your reality. The way it is created is how you wake up and live your day. What do you take in? What do you do about it? Most of you do not think on purpose, create on purpose—you just do. You wake up, live your day, go to sleep. Wake up, live your day, go to sleep.

Everybody is wanting something; everybody is wanting more or different than they have. Nobody is truly satisfied. No one is truly happy on every subject. If you were, you would not be here, you would have learned everything there is to learn about the world. You are still here. Others, like you, are still here learning about the worlds in a physical body. Your Higher Being is learning about the worlds using a physical, pretend reality. You have Source Beings at your disposal.

You manifest your life, but there are ways for you to do a better job of it. What you think about you get more of, what you love upon you get faster. Add energy work and you can become unstoppable. This is how to create on purpose:

1. Thoughts create things – positivity and then
2. Ask for our help – meditation and verbally

Manifestation of the True Self

3. Root-cleansing activities – Directed Energy within
4. Enjoy your life – exaggerate the positive, add appreciation for all you do

That is all there is to it. That is the manual; I want you to use it. The thing about energy work, the words themselves imply hard. Add joy and make it fun and it will not feel like work. Touchpoint activation, that phrase is less harsh. "I'm taking my second shower, I'm integrating energy cleansing. I am cleaning the Root." You get the idea. Make it seem playful and fun and you will make time for it.

Directed Energy is motion-activated Root chakra cleansing. Motion-activated. When two touchpoints come together it is the On switch to rotate energy forward. Forward, under, up, and over. Forward, under, up, and over. It is a field, a bubble around your bodies. It does not just go forward moving out into the atmosphere—no place to land. It is a boundary around you and it circulates within the boundary. You want it to circulate forward, under, up, and over.

The energy movement is, for all of you, crosswise, erratic, spiking. If you think about a root ball, a tree or a large bush that has been tipped over and you see the gangly knot of roots, it is beautiful. This root structure is enormous; it is amazing to see how life has intertwined itself. We love tree roots. We do not love them in your bodies.

Picture now many of these root balls in your energy field. Enormous, amazing entwined integrated system of energy that is swirling around each other disrupting the pattern of flow that was originally there. It is alive and moving. It is swirling in and out and in and out and in and out. It has tails streaming out of it because new energy is coming in,

Chapter 10 ~ Cleansing the Root Chakra

adding to it.

That is your attractor, drawing to it, drawing to it, drawing to it. These root balls are attracting more like themselves; it is where your inner-mind is getting its information from but also it is where the inner-mind is filing situations that are not pleasing to you. They are getting more gangly by the moment.

The Root simply has a label on it that says "Stop!" plus a subject and that becomes what you draw to you. You want those Root balls to be removed. You can make them smaller. We can remove them.

When you integrate Root-cleansing, you shift the energy around the strings that are hanging out of each and every Root ball. When you shift the energy it takes what is coming in (the positive frequency), gathers it up, and softens the knot. It is like adding oil to a knot of hair to loosens the strands so the knot can be unwoven.

It is the same. Source frequency removes the knots. Your positivity in general softens all knots. Your positivity on specific subjects softens and reduces the knots on that subject. It is a cleansing. It is an On switch. It is like a windshield that never gets wet in the rain while it is activated. Consistent activation retrains the entire chakra system on how to be less prone to negative energy from the world, dense thoughts, and ugly behaviors that do not serve you nor others.

We focus on the Root because that is where dense energy lands. It is not gravity, but you can imagine it that way. It does not make you heavy because it is there. However, if you have gotten fat, then you have knots (beliefs) of wellness around physical things. The Root is not baggage. It is a portion of the invisible you.

It is lovely, it is beautiful, this invisible you, but it is supposed to be clean. You would love what this part of you did for you if you cleaned it consistently, because it magnifies your thoughts and eventually creates something that can be experienced from them.

The entire system of your energy field is clogged. The knots themselves form in the Root. Depending on what they are, they may shift or float to a landing place throughout this invisible bubble (energy field) and lodge themselves somewhere and then you stop getting things. Manifesting or maintaining your life becomes challenging or impossible.

How many of these Root balls do you have? Do not worry about it. Do not compare your life to someone else's and say they must have a cleaner or dirtier energy body. They might not. Your unique Soul Intentions also form the basis of your life. You have to take all of this in. It is the secret you have been asking for. It is not simple A+B, but more akin to A+B+C+D+E+F+G, these facets that go into whether you are able to create on purpose. For simplicity, I say thoughts + emotions + energy work. The added complexity is that many thoughts surface at once.

You are a spirit Being incarnate. That Being has laid the foundation of your life by bringing forward aspects of living. From that, certain things are known by your Soul Within (inter mind). Your physical body is chosen and you arrive here in the world through a mother. You are influenced from that moment forward. You have forgotten that you have an exterior you that you cannot see and that you are supposed to

Chapter 10 ~ Cleansing the Root Chakra

be showering it using energy techniques just as you do your skin with soap bubbles. You simply grow up dirty-fielded.

Soul Intentions can be anything—except harmful. I lay this out for you so that you understand the big picture. Some of you are more logic-minded and you need that. I want you to know that this foundation, Soul Intentions, is what your Higher Self is wanting to learn from the physical world. They are learning how to be enthusiastic without their full awareness. It is a fun experience for that Being. They are wanting you to realize this fully and explain it to others who are interested in mindful living, Source-living.

When you learn the foundational information about conscious living, you awaken to the Truth (capital T) of the duality that each of you are experiencing. When you understand this, the inner-mind releases its hold on the belief that it has formed your being. It is this belief that is the largest Root ball that you have.

Once something is understood by the ego mind it resides there eternally and can come forward when activated in future lifetimes. Its current understanding is that it is responsible for your life, that it is your creator, that it is functioning properly. It is not. Your Guide is your co-creator. The egoic self, the inner-mind, is your attractor. The inner-mind does not have awareness of your Guide. That is what we are teaching it. When it learns this, it will allow your Guide to bring experiences to you that satisfies your dreams and desires.

Peace does not flow like a river—it is supposed to, but it does not currently in your world. Peace can settle on you and becomes who you are. Peace is supposed to flow like a river—which is a beautiful metaphor for the river of Source frequency within your energy field. The peace river has boulders instead of soft sand as its base. Remove the boulders, water flows smoothly. When you think of it that way, it does feel better, or does it not?

For those of you with aura sight, the Root chakra ought to be red unless you have an aspect of a past life as one of your Soul Intentions. In that instance, it will be magenta as far as your color wheel goes. It gets darker, they all do, the more knots are present. Cleansing the Root chakra lightens it up. When it is lighter, you feel lighter.

How do you do it? There are many ways. Uprooting is the first exercise I describe to you. Running the energy is number two. Centerline maintenance is number three.

CHAPTER 11

Grounding Explained

*Grounding roots you in the world.
The world is heavy, it is dense,
it plants you where you are.
If you ground too often,
you will find less satisfaction in life, not more.*

Chapter 11 ~ Grounding Explained

Session: 11, video #0713
Date: November 20, 2021, 1:14 p.m.

We had a lengthy pause a moment ago because Carol's inner-mind needed healing from envy. We are on this cruise for eight days, seven nights in the Caribbean, stopping at three ports. At sea two days straight at a time, at the beginning and at the end. We are nearing completion of her cruise and nearing completion of the second book for the cruise, book three overall. Envy cropped up because she is pulled between finishing dictation for this book and laying in the sun, enjoying the last day on the ship. Duality exposes limitations. Limitations are emotions that cause reduced joy. The limitation I identified in her a moment ago was envy, so I addressed it. She is now more patient and comfortable with doing this activity.

When a human being says yes, I will do what is asked of me then they get to do it, whatever it is. When the human being makes time for it, then it gets done. These books that I am writing through her are what I intended to write. I am writing not only about realities, but healing. I am a teacher. I teach how to heal the world and your physical bodies, which helps you manifest better lives for all of you that choose to do the work.

Uprooting this is Carol's favorite activity. It is not a new-age term for grounding. It is far different and much better for you. Grounding has its place, but do not overuse it. I teach you grounding first on the way to uprooting. Grounding is not a Root-cleansing exercise, but it is information that I want you to know so you do not confuse the two.

Grounding is used for physical balance in the moment. If you are a ballerina, use it, for it will cause you to be steady vertically. If you have inner-ear problems and have bouts of dizziness, use it, for it will steady you vertically. If you have symptoms of vertigo and you experience the wave sensation or worse, use it, for it will balance you vertically or remove vertigo altogether. If you are a yogi or aspiring to be one, use it, for it will help you in your poses. It will not help strength, but it will help with balance.

Keeping your eye on a dot-point on the wall as you twirl is a technique that people have used to create vertical steadiness. Grounding is its replacement. How often do you do it? Depending on what is going on with you, never. If you have no balance problems, if you are not looking to be a yogi, if you are steady on your feet, if you are not a ballerina or have no problems with balance, you do not need it.

Grounding roots you in the world. The world is heavy, it is dense. Grounding plants you where you are. If you ground too often, you will find less satisfaction in life, not more. You will be able to manifest fewer things. You will not move forward in your life. You might not get promotions because promotions are forward motion. Forward motion slows down when you ground, it roots you where you are mentally. I do not mean this in a metaphoric way.

With these cautionary notes, I am willing to teach this to you grounding. If you are captivated or enjoy the visualness of this work, I will help you to not lose sight of what it is used for. Your focus on the details is good and will get better over time. Its usefulness remains the same, forever. It is physical balance that is the result, always.

Chapter 11 ~ Grounding Explained

Sit with eyes closed. Let the air around you get still. Breathe in, breathe out softly, not too deep, not too shallow. Let the air slow down like waves in a pool. The splashing has stopped. Water has slowed down. Slower still. Slower still. The white caps have stopped. Stillness starting. Stillness is what you want to feel. Stay there a moment. Let your heart rate slow as well. Feel peaceful inside. When you do, allow your mind to drift to your feet first, hands second.

Let your feet become heavy. So heavy in fact, that they slip through the ground into the Earth. Growing longer and longer until they are deep within the Earth and land on rock that is steady and grow around the rock formations. Let your hands follow your feet. Your arms are simply growing longer until they reach the same rock formation. Grasp it. Fingers and thumb growing all the way around until you are holding on with feet and hands around the rock within the Earth.

Stay there for two minutes breathing semi-deep, yet slowly. Soft inbreath, soft out breath. Then simply let go of the rock formation, hands first. As the hands recede upward back towards the physical body, allow the toes and the feet to unlatch from the rock formation and gently follow the hands until you feel them as their natural length. Stretch out your fingers and your toes. Move your wrists and ankles about, then shake them or massage them so that your mind feels that your hands and feet are both connected, no longer elongated.

Eyes still closed, rub the inner part of your eyes where it connects with your nose gently downward, lift off, down again, lift off, down again. It is a gentle pressing down. 12 to 15 times and then the same at the outer corner of each eye. You may do this with two hands, one on each eye at the same time. Press and pull down, release. Press and pull down, release. Then again behind your ear above the ear lobe. Press and pull down, release. Press and pull down, release. Alongside the shape of the ear is good. Straight down is not quite as good, but is okay.

When finished, allow the fingertips to move along the ears down the jaw along the jaw line until they come together at the base of the chin. Release. Touch your forehead, fingers together where the scalp and hair meet your forehead. Draw two lines coming straight down your nose, the underside of the nose, the upper lip, over both lips down to the chin where you initially released. Breathe in nice and deep. Exhale fully so that there is no more air remaining in your lungs. Simply open your eyes and you are finished. Do this finger placement sequence immediately following the grounding exercise, however it can be used more often if you have balance issues.

If you have bouts of imbalance, prevention is good. Once a day or every other day. This exercise roots you to the position of upright. It also roots you in position— of where you are. Do not overuse this technique—or any grounding technique—that you might come across. It could backfire on you and keep you from moving forward in life. Relationships can fail because of it. Health can fail because of it. Jobs cannot move forward or fail because of it. Feeling dissociated from the world, friends and family, your normal routine can occur because of it. But it is useful—I am not contradicting myself here—it is useful for vertigo, balance impairments, and the like, but caution must be exercised on

Chapter 11 ~ Grounding Explained

the length and frequency of it.

This is a technique rooted in our Knowing with how the worlds work. It is not false, imagination, or made-up. The energy points within the feet and the toes and the palms of the hands, when they connect through your vision with rock formations in the Earth, you are moving to that location. There is much that you do not understand about this reality that you are experiencing. Energy is the way of everything. Your mind will travel to the Earth and you will find balance there. Your minds can learn too quickly and return you to that position. That position is rooted in what you call space and what you call time.

If you see the same rock formation again and again, do not continue because your mind is halting you from moving forward in life. If you see different rock formations, you may continue.

CHAPTER 12

Uprooting:
Root-Cleansing Activity 1

*As I said, we are pure love.
Purity of love and nothing else.
When we create, when we make, when we do,
when we think, when we bond,
it can only contain love, for it is what we are
and we create in the likeness of ourselves.*

Chapter 12 ~ Uprooting: Root-Cleansing Activity 1

Session: 11, video #0713
Date: November 20, 2021, 1:35 p.m.

There are different ways of initiating touchpoint activation—healing, in other words—of the Root chakra. Some of them use physical touch, some of them use visual touch. All of them are working the kinks out of the knots in the Root. Uprooting is a Root-cleansing activity and the very best to use, so I offer it to you first.

Unlike grounding, uprooting can and should be used daily or as often as you like. There is no limitation for you with it. It harmonizes the energy within the etheric. Uprooting can keep you from getting sick, keep you from aggravating people, keep you from negativity or indecision, or keep you awake longer, with less fatigue. The knots in the Root soften from doing it, even occasional use is better than nothing. Any alteration you can do to the knots is good for you. This list is just a sampling, do not take it as an exhaustive.

The world as you know it is a large rock formation. Gems, stones, oil, minerals, water, elements, atmospheric pressure, cloud formations, precipitation, trees, mountains, plants, animals, people. When I say the world, I am talking about Earth. The Earth itself was formed by those that create worlds. It is a job? Is it a fun thing to do? It sure is. Do we create a world by ourselves? No we do not. We form together, we band together. We do it as a group. It is idea creation first, and the completion of it is done by many. And, yes, I have participated in each and every one.

As I said, we are pure love. Purity of love and nothing else. When we create, when we make, when we do, when we think, when we bond, it can only contain love, for it is what we are and we create in the likeness of ourselves. It is what that phrase means. When we create a world, it vibes love. There is a frequency, a tone that is built-in that is love. That frequency and tone is healing by nature because it was created by nonphysical Beings, specifically those who do that job. The frequency of us is built-in, put it that way.

Uprooting is not the opposite of grounding; it is altogether different. It is the uprooting of dense thoughts. The name gives you a good visual. When you uproot a weed, you are removing it completely. When you uproot, you are doing the same thing. You are cleaning out the outermost layer of your Root chakra. That is wise for you to do often. I suggest whenever you are preparing meals, whenever you are brushing your teeth, whenever you are arriving somewhere. Make it a habit whenever you park your car.

Do it often enough that it becomes second nature, and that outer layer stays crystalline. Crystalline is better than clean—it is crystal-clear. You can have clean or crystal-clean. You want crystal-clean. When you uproot often you will see the positive effects emotionally first, then in areas of your life in order of difficulty, with the easiest first. The length of time to acquire crystalline is different for all of you because the Root chakra is unique to you. However, in general do this activity daily at a minimum as a practice.

Uprooting is using Earth energies, Source energy, that is infused in the planet, so to speak. It is soaking in the energies of Source via the rock. Wherever you are, there is rock beneath you. If you are standing on a boat in the deepest part of the ocean, there is still rock beneath you.

Chapter 12 ~ Uprooting: Root-Cleansing Activity 1

The distance does not matter. It soaks in anywhere, at any time, through the bottoms of your feet as well as the palms of your hands. You may do them all at one time or one by one. The right foot aids the right side, the right-hand aids the front. The left foot aids the left side, the left-hand aides the back. There is no need for top and bottom because those four sides intersect at both.

Sit anywhere you like in any position. Similar to meditation, be as comfortable as possible, wherever you are, not too hot, not too cold. If you feel not quite right sitting upright with feet on the ground, for example, try curling up in the couch and wrapping up loosely in a blanket. The mind likes to be cocooned often.

NOTE ABOUT COCOONING: Forethought for those with children or those that have them in your life's path. Having a sheet in your living room is good for small children instead of a blanket. The thin layer resembles their memory of being swaddled as an infant and creates a soothing, security effect that calms the mind. By mid-teens, if not done early in life, the memory of swaddling will fade and the opportunity for its use will be lost. If done young in life, the swaddling memory can be used for physical healing. If used often, lifelong perhaps, it will settle the stomach first, then the arms, then the feet, then joints, ears eyes nose and mouth go together, throat and esophagus next, internal organs last. Swaddling is good. Cocooning as an adult it is also good.

For uprooting, if you swaddle or cocoon yourself do it loosely because the body might feel the energy moving, and if it does, it might activate a memory of a heat register or hot air (depending on where you grew up) and you might become warm. Cocoon softly, but be able to loosen it to remove your arms to cool the body temperature down, should that occur.

Close your eyes when you are in position. Use imagery here and feel for the bottom of your feet and/or hands. Be aware of the toes and where they connect to the foot. Be aware of the shape of the foot all the way to the heel. Be able to take an imaginary finger and trace the bottom of your foot all around the exterior, back up and between each toe. That identifies for the inner-mind the area of your energy field that you are wanting it to focus on. Do that one foot at a time and then for each palm.

When you have finished, picture a circle on each palm and each foot. Allow the circle to open. There is nothing more that you need to do besides watch in your mind's eye what happens next. There will be a cord or a flowing upwards through the circle, up your limbs, along your skeletal structure. It will move in the direction of your chakra layers, Root to Crown and then back down. It will follow the path down the same as it went up.

When it reaches the beginning point simply close the circle. Wait for all four to be closed. Then begin pressing inward at the innermost corner of the eye, where it meets the nose. Press and hold for 17 seconds, and release. Press the outer corner of the eye for 17 seconds and release. You may do one at a time or both simultaneously. It is, of course, fastest to do both at the same time. There is nothing gained by doing one by one. Press behind the ear, not the lobe but the skin on the head where it meets the ear. Preciseness is not necessary. Above the lobe, below the top of the ear, but

Chapter 12 ~ Uprooting: Root-Cleansing Activity 1

in the back.

Trace all the way down the ear, the upper jaw, the lower jaw, until your fingers meet at the base of your chin. Do not remove them or release. Move upward along the chin, the lips, the underside of the nose, over the nose up the forehead all the way to the back of the neck, around the neck and back up to your starting position.

There is no need to go under the hairline. It is always best to not worry about such things. Over the hair and up is just fine. It is better that way. Do not concern yourself with the trivialities of the world and having messy hair. I want you to understand this.

The line that is being drawn creates a barrier so that the energies stay within your etheric and does not leak out. You get the maximum effect of healing when you do this. If you stop and release and press again underneath your hair and then back up, you have stopped the barrier wherever your fingers separated from your scalp. Up and over, keep in contact the entire time all the way back to your starting position behind the ear. Then simply open your eyes and breathe and move on with your day.

How often can you do this? As often as you remember to. You do not have time to not do it. It is that important in your life, alongside meditation. Uprooting is your best friend in this life. There is no need for a logbook entry. There is no need to keep track of how often unless you find it fun to keep track of it. Do not be judgmental or critical if you miss a day or an afternoon. Consistency is key, but do not be overly demanding. Rigidness is not helpful. It will not hurt you should you miss a moment to uproot. It is just a beautiful activity of healing. Do not cloud it with the messiness of guilt.

NOTE: Carol, at the time of putting the manuscript together, asks me about the barrier and why it is at the head only. I want you to understand that the inner-mind does know where Root and Crown are. When you start at the Root it knows the beginning point. When you soak in the energies it flows upward, in a very real way it follows the path of less density. Crown, of course, is your least dense chakra point. By creating a barrier at the head, up and around as I described, the barrier identifies the Crown for the inner-mind. It is a way of marking the uppermost area that will contain Source frequency.

She asks again, "What about the arms/?"—the elbows come to mind for her as well as the shoulders. It is simple for all of you to understand that she too is a person learning from hearing. As we compile the manuscript, she stopped me and asked to go for one of our "walk and talks" so I could explain it to her. She desperately wants to understand the material so she can confidently present it to her publisher who will then put the material in your hands. She is fearful of adding myth or misconception to the world's understanding of energy healing.

I am proud, yet not, of her questions. I want her to know the material is always a portion of the whole. I want her to ask questions to receive more, for the fun of knowing these things, and not add in the factor of the potential that she has mistyped or added punctuation incorrectly, thereby changing the meaning. I reminded her again that by reading out loud, with me, and her High Guide, the errors in auto-translation are all removed.

Chapter 12 ~ Uprooting: Root-Cleansing Activity 1

Precise she is, an energy seeker she is, and so her desire for complete understanding is the true driver of her questions. She asked me again, this time without the unconfident tone and she recognized that her question altered itself, had shifted from "But why?" to "But what if...?" I like that best. It is curiosity that I want to see in her and in each of you. So I explain with added detail, if I were to guide you to create the barrier at the elbow, the inner-mind would assume the Crown is at that level, which is merely at the height of your mid-torso. This would negate half of the uprooting exercise because the inner-mind would ignore the fresh frequency that was brought into the full spectrum of the energy field. The barrier needs to be at the uppermost portion. The reason for tracing the full face and head as I described is because it is the base of the Crown chakra.

As each of you read this material and come upon paragraphs or even whole chapters that are not understood, keep reading the book. Get all the way to the end. Some things are explained in successive chapters. I form the basis of understanding, lay out the topics, and then discuss one by one. Should you still feel confused, then set the book aside for a month, mark the areas of confusion without highlighting—a bookmark will do. Meditate as you usually do (daily, hopefully) and then go back and re-read the section that left you questioning what I meant. More will be understood. Meditation, I cannot stress enough, if done daily as a silent practice, cures, as it helps you slow your thinking down enough for your High Guide to intuit meaning to you—then you suddenly "get it." I like these additions; they are helpful to all of you.

CHAPTER 13

Running the Energy: Root-Cleansing Activity 2

*Your High Guide is the one giving you a visual to use
and they always choose the one
that is easiest for your mind to conjure.
Give yourself love by appreciating their involvement.
It will aid you.*

Chapter 13 ~ Running the Energy: Root-Cleansing Activity 2

Session: 11, video #0713
Date: November 20, 2021, 2:15 p.m.

The second exercise, running the energy, is good to do as often as you like. This one begins with the feet. Focus on the bottoms, trace the outer edge of the foot and then the toes, as you did with uprooting. Find the center-point of the sole of your feet which would be the center of the circle that you used in uprooting. When you find it, open it, your intuition will guide you. It might appear in your mind's eye as a trap door, it might be a cut-out that is set aside but not lost track of. It could be double doors or anything that latches completely shut.

Your High Guide is the one giving you a visual to use and they always choose the one that is easiest for your mind to conjure. Give yourself love by appreciating their involvement. It will aid you. When that spot is opened it will begin drawing energy from us. It may come from any direction and find the sphere. There will be a pulling or drawing-in motion. It might feel like a wisp of smoke. It might feel like a thread being drawn upward. It will be narrow, it will be soft, it will be gentle, it will be softly cleansing the Root.

Your High Guide is doing the work of this activity but it is good for you to pay attention to how much the mind is showing you about what is being done. Some of you have excellence in your perception ability. You might feel the energy stopping and pulsing, you might feel it swirl. You might feel it swiftly move up and then stop and pulse. You may feel an up and down motion. They are all meaningful.

What you are wanting to see is a drawing up, similar to "tissues" that are connected. There's an endless supply, and you keep selecting one after another, after another, after another, after another.

The movement of the energy will go up your skeletal structure, up the legs, up the spine, up the neck, around or through the face and then back down to the feet. What you are experiencing is a cleansing activity from your High Guide. They are traveling from Root to Crown, activating each point along the proper path for you. The general path is the same for all, with slight differences individually. Your path is your own because of your Birth (Soul) Intentions, which simply means there are some things that are built-in and do not need cleansing. If so, your High Guide will skip them altogether. You will not know it, but it is good information for you to have.

The right foot aids the left side in this activity. Left foot aids the right side. The two touch at top and bottom. Although your mind might show you energy going up the right leg from the right foot, the healing that has occurred is so the left side can draw healing to it from the right. The same with the opposite side. The right side will draw healing to it from the left, and it will create balance. Not vertical balance, but emotional balance.

You do not need to use your hands for this exercise, your mind will do it automatically. As your core is cleansed, it will filter down all the way to the fingertips. You might perceive movement to the hands and back up again. If you do, that is excellent. It means that you have excellent perception of where the energy, where the healing, is flowing.

Chapter 13 ~ Running the Energy: Root-Cleansing Activity 2

When it flows back down to the starting point at the bottom of the feet, simply allow the High Guide, at their leisure, to close off that opening. The visual will be given to you. It could be that the cutout is placed back in and smoothed over with a hand. It could be a gentle clasp of a locket. It could be gently, the quiet closing of a door.

Allow the mind to feel what your High Guide is offering to it. You are the bystander watching the healing occur. You are watching a conversation that your High Guide is having with your physical body by way of allowing energy to flow upwards from the Earth into your physical form through your limbs and then sealed so that the cells of your body may then use it.

This is healing that occurs. The natural state memory of each cell goes far deeper than the cell that you see in a microscope—about fourteen layers deeper. It refreshes and renews the memory of wellness and it heals from within. Over time, that cellular memory is so strong that everyday life and the occurrences of negative influence will not upset its balance and you stay healthy.

NOTE: Carol asks me to explain whether uprooting and running the energy are the same exercise just explained differently. I said, "Yes, but also no." These walks and talks are good to gather the uncertainties she, herself, has with it.

I am her Teacher in the nonphysical and her Higher Self is pleased when she asks questions. Yours is as well. This is so important for each of you to grasp. Your Higher Self is participating in your life. They are concentrated intently on what you are doing. Beyond that, each time you gather us to you and gain Knowledge, they expand. It is not too far different than your board games. If you think of it this way and find enjoyment in it, then you have little to no resistance in believing that you are a nonphysical Being having a life experience in a sub-reality that is perception-based.

Let's say the above sentence makes sense to you. Your Higher Being gets a point and moves forward two steps. When you are drawn to a book like this one they get no points but are eager to find out whether you will actually read it. They intuit to you, "Read it, please, I get to advance another square." You are like their invisible partner in a classroom learning exercise.

When you read the book that you picked up—one of substance I mean here; metaphysics in general do count but the squares are much smaller. If it is a channeled work the material is Knowledge and substantial to your learning. The game squares triple in size. You get the idea.

Now, uprooting is an exercise that is of a healing nature for the Root chakra, as is running the energy. They both include using the openings in the feet—you could say portals and would be accurate enough for this level of your learning. They both draw in or soak up Source frequency infused within the world in the rock of your planet.

The uprooting requires a barrier identifier at the Crown, running of the energy does not. The question Carol is really asking is what is different between the two. Again, remove all traces of uncertainly, of doubt, of questioning, and be open to curiosity. It aids your ability to harness the power of positivity in a learning environment and, by way of it, understand the material better. Your Higher Self moves forward one space.

In the uprooting exercise you are focused on watching

Chapter 13 ~ Running the Energy: Root-Cleansing Activity 2

the energy move upward and back down. Watching the energy takes concentration. It will be shown to you by way of intuition. The barrier is needed so the frequency of Source stays within the boundary and is not ignored by the inner-mind—that is what I meant as "leaking." Remember here, the inner-mind and you are focused together on watching the energy, not what is being done with it.

In the running of the energy exercise, you are being shown what your High Guide is doing with the Source frequency. It is why you may see it swirl or pulse or pause. When it does, your High Guide is working on soothing one or more knots. Keep watching when it does and you will witness more healing occurring. The healing is being done nonetheless, but the more you are aware of the more the inner-mind holds onto.

In essence, the exercises are different mental focuses. Uprooting—the soaking up of the energy only. Running of the energy—what your High Guide is doing with it.

In private sessions with me (or The Jeshua Collective, as would be the case), Carol would be in her usual trance state and we would verbalize to you through her what she is being shown about your energy session. She sees past, present, and future "scenes," as well patterns of behavior that are being touched on. It is good to have these types of individual sessions because the inner-mind learns as you do—verbally. When you do the exercises on your own you do receive good amounts of healing. It is also good to have the verbal component so that you know which knots were soothed so that you can expect certain changes. We explain in detail what the outcome is, complete/incomplete, and what is on the forefront for you because of it.

CHAPTER 14

Directing Energy Maintenance Sequences

*Believing in energy healing is a very good thing
that you can do for yourself.
Teaching it to others is a very good thing
that you can do for them.
When it is taught by the Guides
through a person who is channeling our words,
our Knowing, it is the very best for all.*

Chapter 14 ~ Directing Energy Maintenance Sequences

Session: 12, video #0714
Date: November 20, 2021, 2:37 p.m.

It is still November 20, 2021, at 2:37 p.m. It is beginning to rain. Carol took a little bit of time in between video sessions and went out on the balcony. It is a decent-sized one. She moved the lounge chairs over to one side and then moved the captain's chairs also over to one side. Then she laid a towel down and allowed us to move her. She had the sensation that she had been sitting for too long. She generally knows when we are intuiting to her. This time, she did not stop to ask us a question, she simply got up and moved the furniture.

We want you to remember that. When you have a thought that feels good, go with it. It might be the very thing that you are needing. For Carol, a moment ago it was the need for gentle stretching, some twists and bends of yoga. Standing up and stretching tall and reaching down, moving her limbs from side to side slowly.

Gently stretching is good for you. Your skeletal system needs stretching, however, it is not the muscles that need to be stretched. Your bones and your ligaments are what need tending to—you are moving them back into proper alignment. When you do, the muscles adhere properly and move into proper position again.

Carol had been sitting for quite a while. We had intended nothing for this day specifically, but we asked her to use today in a way that would allow her to feel the best as her vacation concluded. She said, "I want to do three things. I want to participate in a morning activity that she identified

(Sudoku), I want to finish book three (this one) and I want to sit in the hot tub in the rain if they will allow it.

She finds water fascinating. She likes to see it move. She likes to see it fall. She likes to feel it in her hand. She likes water. She likes to be near water, not in it unless it is small and not too deep. As most of you, she prefers it warm. A small, shallow hot tub is what she chose for today. We think she will get there. We also know that the book will be finished before she does it.

It is raining outside at the moment. She has an aft(rear)-facing cabin and she is seeing the fog slowly cover the landscape of the water. The rain is slow but steady. Waves, but nothing scary. Rolling waves, the kind that you would expect. She likes to watch the water move. It is comforting and soothing. She does not like to be in it but she adores cruising. We run the energy constantly so that she enjoys it on the inside. When you do the previous exercise, you witness what we are doing; you are not a cooperative component but the experience of witnessing aids your healing. What you learn, what you enjoy, you get more of.

Twice during this cruise she has needed a nap. One was lengthy, almost three hours. Her eyes got heavy to the point where she knew that her body needed rest. She fell fast asleep—after talking to us, of course—and then woke up almost three hours later feeling refreshed, feeling like she had had a good night's sleep. She was surprised at the time that had lapsed, but not upset about it. Then she did what someone like her does, she asked us this question, "Was that a healing sleep or just regular?" Happy tones in her voice, excited expectation, hopefulness that it was a healing

Chapter 14 ~ Directing Energy Maintenance Sequences

sleep because energy healing fascinates her. She wants it constantly.

Not at her request, but as a complement to her way of life, we gave this information to her—there is nothing that you cannot ask us for. If you can dream it up, we can do it. Healing sleep is not an exercise, it is an asking. I like to call it "partnering up." When you are getting ready to take a nap, ask me to do that thing that I do and fall asleep.

What is that thing that I do? I heal the body. It is your High Guide that is doing it. I am Carol's Highest Guide. She does have one that is between her High Guide and me, and that one is lending their energy to everything she does as well. She has this habit of saying, "I want the most," and she gets it.

She has an awareness that there are levels of Guides and she loves on each one. Recognizes each one. Does that human thing of making sure that no one gets their feelings hurt if she jumps to the Highest for conversation. We do not have feelings so we do not get hurt. Far be it from us to stop you from ever asking for more.

We like it. Everyone lends their energy. It is true that the higher you go, the more you get. Your High Guide knows how to do everything that you are needing. There are things that I do that are different or more-than because I am bigger. When you come upon Knowledge (capital K), meaning teachings from us, we want you to use it.

Your High Guide is the one that creates your Unfoldment Plan. They are the ones that design how you get things and what the path will be. You and that attractor within have a way of cluttering it up, putting obstacles on the path. We teach you how to clear away the obstacles so that there are less of them (reduction in size) and also so there are fewer added to your future (no quantity added).

When Carol asks me to "do that thing that I do" (it is one of her famous phrases with us), it is her way of circumventing making an oops in her asking. Trial and error is how using that phrase came to be. She would ask for a certain thing, try to describe it, and find that she would get twisted with her thoughts. She would feel guilt or bad or remorse or doubt. She simply waved her hand in the air one day and said, "That didn't feel right, just do that thing that you do." It was a giving-up action that worked for her. She smiled and said that phrase felt good, felt lighter, felt like she did not have to work hard at asking me for something. So she uses it as well as "More of that, please."

Sometimes less is more.

When a human being comes upon a phrase that feels good when they are talking to us and because of us, we are proud of you. Know that if you have gotten this far in this book, you have many eyes that are on you from the nonphysical world helping you to understand it, to keep going. Your High Guide is doing energy healing on you the entire time that you are reading so that your inner-mind can pay attention to the tones that are underneath the words. When it relaxes, your understanding of the words increases.

Your High Guide and all of those that are assigned to you are not bystanders. They are always sending different tones to the body to do something, to fix something, to heal something, to remind you of something, to give you something, to bring something to you, to keep something

Chapter 14 ~ Directing Energy Maintenance Sequences

going, or to slow something down. There are many and they are at work twenty-four/seven for your entire life. Your High Guide is the mastermind of the guardianship of you. They keep track of your inner-mind and its relationship with the physical world.

We are not needy, meaning we do not need adoration, but your inner-mind learns trust by way of quantity, so in that respect acknowledging that you have us around and loving on us is helpful. Your Guide Team are your co-creators. What you ask for, they bring to you. What you allow in, you get. They keep track of you. They heal you. They prepare the path, clean the path, open up more pathways, and they are side by side with you, placing unceasing attention on you forever.

Forever is forever because the assignment is made at your Being's beginning. As you grow, it grows with you. That is why they are always your senior partner. It is built-in for you to have a partner. Every lifetime, your High Guide is there, and they know everything about everything, about you, about the world, and how to do the job that they are doing.

When you decide to form a bond with that Guide from your physicality or any of the Higher Guides, you add to your own healing as well as your ascension in the nonphysical. Healing is, of course, for the physical.

We can tell you what we do, but if you do not believe in us or of healing from us you receive the full effect anyway. When you trust and understand, your thought patterns change and you create less barriers to receiving in general. Barriers can become insurmountable. Many lives have fallen victim to it. Do not be one that does. You do not need to recognize the signs of aging or illness. You simply need to understand and recognize that you are having a physical life experience and that many things are built-in to help you.

You have a series of Guides, touchpoints within your body, a Conduit of Life, a Conduit of Communication, an energy field and its barrier, energy within your physical body that is of Source, energy within the world that is of Source, the ability to receive intuitively, and the ability to increase intuition to become a medium or channel for guidance given verbally.

Believing in energy healing is a very good thing that you can do for yourself. Teaching it to others is a very good thing that you can do for them. When it is taught by the Guides through a person who is channeling our words, our Knowing, it is the very best for all.

Human beings have imaginations, and there are other examples of our Knowing in the world. What you think about you get more of. When you are interested in the topic, you find more information on it. Almost all information on energy work and intuitive development is written by people based on what they have come across.

"Research says…"—a researcher is focused on a topic by choosing it. Whether he or she believes that they have an intended outcome on their mind or not, they do because of quantities within. They will find evidence for what the internal quantities are suggesting to them.

We are not quantity-based Beings. We are alive. We are knowledge. We are powerful. We are purity. Let this information be what you rely on rather than that which human beings teach each other. Too much gets filtered out

Chapter 14 ~ Directing Energy Maintenance Sequences

because of competition. Rephrasing can make a significant difference between working and not working, healing and not healing.

The exercises and examples that I give are not the only ones I could give. They are the ones I have chosen to bring forward in this particular book. I want you to recognize that. Respect the Teacher and where the teaching comes from and learn to shift away from false teaching, human-straightforward teaching, in favor of Source teaching.

Now, exercise number three is a series of physical touchpoint activations. There are six sequences overall. There is a reason why they are a sequence. It is like a series of waterwheels; if you start with the bottom or the middle, one or more get neglected. If you start at the Crown, you are starting at the top of the water, they all begin to turn—none are neglected. Such is the case with these sequences.

Sequence One – Vertical Meridian

Position one - Right hand or left hand does not matter. There is no better or best. Fingertips or palm are both okay. One hand on the very top of your head or hovering as close as you can. If you have pain in your shoulder or your elbow try the other arm or try resting your arm on a pillow so that it can be above the top of your head. We know some of you have physical ailments. If both arms are in a sling, ask your High Guide to do that one for you. At the same time that one hand is on or above the center of your head, place the fingers or palm of the other hand just above the top of the bridge of the nose, the bottom half of your forehead.

Position two - One hand remains on the top of the head and the other moves down between your breasts. Again, you may touch the skin or hover above it using fingertips or the palm.

Position three - One hand remains on the head and the other moves down to just above the belly button.

Position four - One hand continues to remain on the top of the head and the other moves just below the pelvic bone—hovering just off the skin in the pelvic region just below your torso is what you are reaching for.

Position five - One hand again continues to remain on the top of the head while the other moves to behind your buttocks, to the base of your spine. Sitting on your hand will do.

Hold each of the five positions in sequence, one for a minimum of two minutes. As with all of these sequences, some of you have ocular site. If you do, use it to the best of your ability. Some of you will feel a pulsing or a rhythmic motion just beneath the skin. Some of you will see a line being drawn. Some of you will perceive a lifting up or moving upwards of energy. All are good, some are better than others. If you enjoy watching the perceived energy, do so. When the motion moves up and down, move to the next position. Otherwise use the per-minute method to know when.

Chapter 14 ~ Directing Energy Maintenance Sequences

Sequence Two – Diagonal Left Meridian and Diagonal Right Meridian

This sequence has a left and right component to it. It does not matter which one you do first. It is recommended that you do both. One hand rests on the opposite shoulder, placed casually yet reaching as far as you can. Placement of the hand is midway between the tip of the shoulder and the base of the neck. Place the other hand at the base of your spine and sit on it, or if you prefer to stand simply rest the hand (palm in or out per your comfort level) against the lowest part of your spine. Again, hold two minutes or until you perceive the energies moving straight up and down repeatedly. Then switch and do the other side.

Sequence Three – Diagonal Left and Right Lower Meridian, Interior Thigh

Using the palms for this one, place them on the opposite inner thigh—right hand to left thigh and left hand to right thigh. You can do these both together or one at a time. It makes no difference. Place it on the inside of your thigh. For placement, imagine a line drawn from the center of your inner knee to the top of your inner thigh and place your palm halfway between them.

If your fingers are having a hard time facing the exact same direction and being in the center of your thigh, you are working too hard at it. Just relax and let it be generally comfortable. Fingertips may face in opposite direction. You will know comfort as you do it. Your fingers are not activating anything. The palm is what we want on that centerline of the inner thigh. The fingertips can rest casually.

Some of you have worry within and may believe that you need to hold your fingers off your thigh, it is not necessary to do this. Do not have those kind of worries; they do not help you. Your High Guide is doing the activation, not you, and is using the vortex points in your hands for your self-healing. There is nothing in this life that you do alone, remember this. When you get your hands in position your High Guide begins.

If you cannot reach your thighs, get as close as you can, close your eyes, and perceive a line from that center point of your thigh to the center of the opposite palm. Your ocular vision is real and will connect the touchpoints. Attention to detail is good, but we also want to account for many different sizes and shapes of bodies and not all can reach easily these positions.

We know that sometimes you are in a sling or a cast. Clothing and casts make no difference to energy.

Sequence Number Four – Ankles

Simply cross your legs or put your feet together. Hold your ankle with the palm of your hand covering your inner ankle bone. It is good to do same hand-same ankle (left-left, right-right) as well as opposite hand to ankle (left-right, right-left). Your fingers may wrap around your ankle. You may position them downward and hold the bottom of your feet, whatever is comfortable for you. If it is most comfortable to cross one leg over your knee and do one leg at a time, by all means do it. Find something that is workable for you because if it is, you will create a habit and do it. That is the goal.

Chapter 14 ~ Directing Energy Maintenance Sequences

Sequence Number Five – Diagonal Left and Right Lower Meridian, Outer Thigh

For this one, you will need to reach for the outer thigh. Get as close as you can. Your Guide is very good at what they do and if your hands are slightly off center, do not fret. They know how to angle energy. We do not want you to be lazy about it and just lay on your side doing nothing. But if you are unable to touch the touchpoints one on top of the other, we can do it for you. The reason that we do not want you to be lazy about it is that your mind will create a lazy pathway for the energy. A lazy pathway is narrow and cleansing will be less. When you focus on something, it does it more fully. When you put effort into it, the inner-mind will allow it more fully.

Those things are good. It is not laziness that we are correcting, it is the narrowness of the cord between the touchpoints. Your mind plays a part.

Sequence Number Six – Softens the Mind

The easiest of all, simply take your thumb and place it on top of the nail of your ring finger on the same hand. This one almost all of you can do easily. If your finger is in a cast and therefore cannot bend to reach the thumb of the same hand, you may use the opposite thumb as long as you use the opposite thumb for both hands, even if it is only one finger that is having the problem. It is good to do this at night especially, for then more healing takes place every night as you sleep.

Even though you do not know it we are at work on balancing the major points of your chakra system every single night as you are sleeping. When you do touchpoint activation prior to sleep, then your suite of healer Guides continue where you left off and your inner-mind accepts it. That means you get extra during sleep if you make it a habit of doing the suite of positions, and you understand that you are moving energy in a positive direction. Your attention to detail and understanding of what is occurring always improves the acceptance of the healing activities.

Remind yourself what you are doing and why. We began with information about the inner-mind, that ego mind, the super-attractor within to form the basis of knowledge for you. Do not forget about that. Quantities matter. Quantities are everything. "I am running the energy. I am creating positivity. I am moving energy in a positive direction. I am decluttering the path, taking care of business."

Find a phrase that feels good and create the AND. "I love it AND my Guides are doing it with me. I learned a trick to manifesting AND I am doing what is built-in to cleanse my energy. I am doing it because I like it AND it keeps everything that I'm wanting coming to me quick and easy."

Choose one that you like, just remind yourself of it often. Each of these positions heal different coagulated energy knots that are of a specific type and subject. All of you have these knots—you cannot get away from it in a world where there is density of emotion. We teach you to move away from dense thoughts so you activate positive energy as well.

Coagulation is a term I use to describe what negative ideas, negative thoughts, situations, you name it, do to your energy body. Anything that is opposite of love is subject to finding its way into your chakra system. Anything that does

Chapter 14 ~ Directing Energy Maintenance Sequences

slows down your ability to receive from us—physically (your ability to manifest), or emotionally (your ability to handle situations), or conversationally (your ability to connect with us verbally). While you do not want these knots to occur, it is not undoable. When you tend to them regularly, you see life from a perspective of clarity.

More helpfulness—I hope you are highlighting or taking notes for use when you complete this chapter.

> Stale thoughts, meaning you are finding it difficult to get off a subject is an indicator that you need to do the vertical sequence.

> Forgetfulness is an indicator that you need to do the diagonal sequences.

> Uptight, anxious, nervous, or afraid is an indicator that you need to do sequences one, two, and three.

> Feelings of sadness, regret, remorse, grief, or depression are indicators that you need to do sequences four, five, and six.

It is recommended that you simply do all of them once a day to keep you from any of these emotions and situations.

End chapter.

CHAPTER 15

Quantity-less

*We do get something
out of you keeping your energy field clean as well—
conversation with you!
We get to have more conversations with you.
We get to have more accuracy
from your conveyance of our conversation with you.
I like that, and so does your High Guide.*

Chapter 15 ~ Quantity-less

Session: 13, video #0715
Date: November 20, 2021, 3:32 p.m.

We are still on the ship and doing these chapters in consecutive order during the last full day of this journey. It is a good little rain happening outside. Carol has the veranda sliding glass door half open, curtains wide open, looking outside, watching the rainfall. She took a moment to step outside; she did not like her hair flying around, nor the raindrops, particularly on her face. Mostly, though, it was the hair that made her want to come back inside.

Then she received a thought, an image, and said, "Oh, I have an umbrella." She grabbed it and went back outside, popped it open and stood out there for a while longer, enjoying the view. She remarked that the waves were not much bigger and that it was just raining. She shook off the water from the umbrella, came inside, and then I said, "Are you ready?" She asked if I was getting ready to finish the book.

In those four minutes quantity was added.

She is enjoying looking at the water. She does not know which quantities are being added while she does. I want you all to assume that positive quantities are being added. Look at something and love it. "I love the water. I love the ocean. I love when it rains and I love being outside and I love being inside." Create the AND. "I love the waves that are softly rolling. I love cruising."

In the brief moment that we spoke about what she was doing and mentioned the waves and the rain, it took no time at all for her mind to go down a rabbit hole of movies and add "afraid." She does not feel afraid, but a thought or a memory about ships on the ocean in the rain came to mind. The inner-attractor brought it to her using sight—the image-maker activated and she saw a picture in her mind's eye. It added quantity—or would have if, I was not speaking through her or tending to her energy levels.

Fear is something you all deal with because it is in the world that you are taught to watch television mostly. Afraid is an emotion borne of fear, not of love. When you are feeling afraid, move away from the thought. Simply distract yourself—blink and turn your head. Find something pleasing to look at and then say something like, "Oh, I didn't know that was sitting there. I love that book or that purse, I should put that away."

Make something up. Move off the subject. When you do it quickly, the mind will not add a quantity. How quickly should you do it? Within sixteen or seventeen seconds, depending on how clean your energy is. For almost all of you, seventeen. It is not an absolute meaning—it is not built into this world for it to be that way, but it is evolvement. It is what has been created. It is the way it is for now in your world. Accept it and then do something to counteract it.

When something is bothering you, move on to something else quick and easy and no quantity is registered in the filing cabinet. Your thought pattern on the original subject is still where you left it and will need cleaning up, but do what you can do. I do not want you to consume your lives with cleaning your thoughts or thinking about how much you need to clean your thoughts because that in itself will create a reality of needing more things cleaned up. Unless

Chapter 15 ~ Quantity-less

you create the AND while doing it.

What AND can you create? "I'm doing the energy work so I stay crystal-clear." This one, true, it does get you some of both. You are acknowledging you need energy work but also forecasting that you are crystal-clean. It does have a focus on needing energy work which tells the inner-attractor that you have issues with pizza sauce on your white jeans, for example. But when you say, "I am doing the energy work so I stay crystal-clear" AND you add positive emotion while doing it, your inner-attractor must look at your emotions then add the subject, in that order.

Your most recent focus gets attention first and then in receding order. Happy emotion first, energy work second, and then pizza sauce on your white jeans last. Because dripping pizza sauce is last it might not get registered at all! That means you did not add quantity to the potential of ruining your white jeans in that way.

This is the best explanation for why your statement of appreciation ought to be a longer free-flow of ideas. You could exhaust the momentum to the point where it does not reach your negative subject.

When you distract yourself in the moment, if it is fast and quick from the time you registered unease, no quantity is added. The time it takes to register that something negative is on your mind is something for you to consider. When you find yourself staring off at space thinking or imagining something that is frightening, how long were you doing it? Quantities might have been added.

It is always a good idea to uproot in that moment so the uppermost layer of the etheric field can be "washed" off. It takes but a moment. It is healthy, it is good. It is preventative as well as corrective.

We do get something out of you keeping your energy field clean as well—conversation with you! We get to have more conversations with you. We get to have more accuracy from your conveyance of our conversation with you. Your intuition will skyrocket. Your timing will become excellent. Your mornings will feel fresher. Your afternoons will feel smooth. Your evenings will feel relaxed. Your emotions will have simmered.

Picture a pot of boiling water bubbling, bubbling, bubbling. When you turn off the heat the bubbles slow down until they are nonexistent. The water is at that moment still, but hot. Do not touch it. When the pot sits there for long enough, the temperature of the water cools.

It is the same with your emotions. Cleansing of the Root cools your emotions. It takes longer for anger to erupt like a boiling pot of water. Without Root-cleansing, your emotions are more like a rolling boil—or hot water that is on the edge of boiling. Not hot and cold, hot and less hot. Equate hot to stress levels. Equate stress levels to illness and lack mindset in your reality.

I want you to look at the topics in this book, the ideas I have shared with you, and create a list of them outside of the book. Take it with you, and use them. Know which to use and when. Uprooting is always recommended going into a new situation, coming out of a bad situation, experiencing traffic and finding annoyance in it, shopping and running late to pick up your take-out—the variety of life is so beautiful. Your experiences can be as well, no matter their nature.

Chapter 15 ~ Quantity-less

It is your life. Perhaps I do like the phrase YOLO (You Only Live Once). While not exactly Reality from our nonphysical perspective, it is in fact how you perceive it from your physical awareness. How will you tend to yours? Make a list, check it twice or thrice. Take it with you. Use it. Share it. Do it.

End chapter.

CHAPTER 16

Stoppage Indicators

*Your beliefs are stoppages.
The stoppages are an accumulation of thoughts
that have knotted together.
The knotting occurs in the Root and
they lodged somewhere along your chakra system.*

Chapter 16 ~ Stoppage Indicators

Session: 14, video #0716
Date: November 20, 2021, 3:46 p.m.

I am wanting all of you to know that we are Real. We, those of us here in the nonphysical dimension that includes that part of you that remains here, all of your Loved Ones that are no longer in the physical, any person that you can think of. We are all alive. We have plans and we do things.

So it is with you as well. You are in the physical world. Part of you is experiencing life in a perceived environment, that is the physical world. Life, as you know it, is not real. It is an experience that your Higher Self is having. Your thoughts matter. Your energy levels are an accumulation of your thoughts. Your relationships, your bank account, your love life, the size of your home, the amount of joy in your lives—are an accumulation of thoughts.

Those thoughts that are not helpful accumulate faster by way of attraction. Attraction grows by way of life experience. It is an accumulation of thoughts that have mattered for one reason or another to the aspect of your mind that keeps track of life. That aspect is law of attraction.

It is person by person, lifetime by lifetime. There is no rollover from one lifetime to the next in badness. Evil entities do not exist, except in your earthborn imaginations. The world does not need more storytelling about badness on any topic to any degree, to anyone, including self-talk. Negative self-talk is the number one problem within your chakra's Root. Watch how it changes—in thirty, sixty, ninety, one hundred twenty days. Watch how your thought patterns change for the better by doing these sequences, reframing your thoughts, and other methods described in this book regularly.

Combined, you can hit the restart button on your lives. Healing by your High Guide and healing by way of thought removal is available to you. Healing in partnership with your High Guide through activating touchpoints is available to you. There is no time-out, there are no blackout dates, there are no expensive retreats and workshops that you need to go to in order to heal your lives. Over time, the sequences given here, and more like them, will correct the accumulation of denseness in the Root.

More negative beliefs are born and distributed to your energy field, where they lodge and reside every day. They form the basis of your life. Physical manifestation of a stoppage is automatic. Once the Root ball reaches stoppage state, it has accumulated energy to it.

By the time you feel the onset of a cough, a stoppage has been activated to the point of becoming a belief. By the time that you have a backache, a stoppage has been activated to the point of becoming a belief. The same goes for your inability to manifest generational wealth, physical things, close ties that are loving and healthy, objects and artifacts that are fun to accumulate.

False communication with your High Guide is included in the error caused by Root stoppages. All of you have beliefs in your energy field. Remember now, your thoughts are the result of your influenced beliefs and your beliefs invigorate your thoughts. You do not know what the exact beliefs are. You do see the world at large. You do see your life as it has manifested in relationship to your beliefs, not with its relationship with the world. Your relationship with the world is a result of your beliefs. Your beliefs are stoppages.

Chapter 16 ~ Stoppage Indicators

The stoppages are an accumulation of thoughts that have knotted together. The knotting occurs in the Root and they lodged somewhere along your chakra system. Where they land is the basis for the events that will occur in your life.

If the Crown is clogged, communication with us will be faulty, inaccurate, or nonexistent, except for necessary intuition.

If the stoppage lands at or near the area of the Third Eye, it matters greatly because it will not allow you to receive cleanly from your High Guide. There are ways around it. When necessary, the Third Eye can be opened or activated. It is at the discretion of your High Guide only. It does not matter how many books or videos or classes you take on the subject. You cannot, nor can any human being at any time, ever activate or open your Third Eye. It is impossible. It is a chakra point that belongs to us and us only. Play or dabble or pretend all you want—the Third Eye remains in the position that your High Guide needs it to be.

What most of you are wanting when you talk about opening the Third Eye is better communication with the spirit realm. Cleaning the Crown will help you but the Third Eye is ours.

When a stoppage is within the Throat chakra many things occur. You may not stand up for yourself, or you may be too outspoken. You may fly off the handle. You may have a speech impediment. But it will have something to do with your actual voice or your willingness to see yourself as important.

When the stoppage lands somewhere within the Heart chakra region, relationships falter, you draw the wrong types of people and the wrong circumstances to you. You may have a hard time getting people to accept your invitations, you may have a challenging time communicating, understanding, or getting your point across. You may have a hard time making or keeping friends. You may simply be someone who suddenly decides Christmas cards are no longer important to send. You suddenly stop returning phone calls as quickly and in doing so lose touch with people that you care for. You may simply have a hard time phrasing things and feel awkward with your inability to convey your thoughts to others. Because of it, you withdraw from social activities.

When a stoppage is within the Solar Plexus region you may feel angry, bossy, and push people around. You become a bully or you succumb to them. Dominance or its opposite manifests.

When the stoppage is within the Sacral system, life in general feels challenging. You cannot make traction. Your outlook is poor. You have a tough time on a variety of subjects. It is your outlook that has diminished but also, specific things can manifest. For women, childbearing problems, obesity, forgetfulness are some. For men, insecurity, frailty physically, or diminished masculinity are some. The list is much broader. Those are some of the more common.

If a stoppage remains in the Root you withdraw from the world. You may attempt suicide or may acquire a habit of conjuring ways to do so, even if you do not attempt it. You may form an opinion that the world would be better off without you. The densest of energies and their thoughts can form when this occurs.

All of these can be reduced, minimized, lightened by consistent chakra cleansing and verbal reframing as a habit. Enjoy the knowing of what you are doing with your cleansing

Chapter 16 ~ Stoppage Indicators

actions so that you do not counteract that very thing that you just cleaned up. Overzealous is not what you are wanting to be. Happy is. The healing that is done is healing. A thread that is removed is removed. If you add a new thread the stoppage might seem untouched or not healed. It has been, but do your personal healing work again.

The verbal component helps greatly in lessening the accumulation of new energy within the Root balls. The Root balls themselves reduce over time with cleansing. It speeds up when you do it as a habit—cellular memory kicks in. The Root ball itself is a living organism. It feels what you are doing, it feels energy activated, and it simply says, "Oh, we're doing the cleansing thing. Let's get on it, everybody. It's time for cleansing," and they all get excited for your energy shower.

It is a fun way to think about it—lighten up! Life is easier than you think. Things are built-in to help. Ask more creative questions and you will get our Knowing. We love you so much. We were wanting you to have happy, healthy lives. We bring you this information in the hopes that you use it and share it. We will be talking to you about more. Your High Guide is watching your chakra system every moment of every single day. Be aware of it. Be aware of the world around you. Take heed in the words of this book, use the techniques, and change your lives. I/We love you all during your physical life and beyond.

We are, forever yours.
Book complete.

Opportunities to Engage with Jeshua

Private Consultations with Jeshua:

Workshops are a great way to receive guidance from Source but sometimes there's nothing like a one-on-one, private conversation for readings and energy work. Jeshua is the collective of nonphysical Teachers that are gentle, wise, and straightforward yet compassionate. With pin-pointed accuracy, they know what you need to know and how to bring clarity to your life. Remove fear and doubt on your ability to manifest love, happiness, and all things in abundance. Available by appointment only.

Workshops with Jeshua:

The Powerfulness of Source Energy – The Four Pillars of Learning

This workshop has been designed as a two-day weekend and five-day cruise workshop series, with both options giving you over fourteen hours of engagement with Jeshua. Each workshop begins with The Foundational Material and how knowing who your Guide is helps your intuitiveness. Day one wraps up with law of attraction and an in-depth study on manipulation of thought using creative wordplay. Day two begins with stretching exercises and why they aid self-healing, followed by an array of touch-point activation methods that anyone can do. The workshop ends with a segment on Intuitive Development and validation on the how, why, and when to reach for guidance. A portion of each segment includes Q&A to ensure you have all the tips, tools, and takeaways to help you live your life On Purpose.

Our Knowing – Conversations with Jeshua

The most powerful teachings on law of attraction and connection with your Guide team available! Designed as a monthly 2-hour online event, Jeshua expands the conversation of law of attraction and the power of positivity by combining it with teachings on natural healing to clear away the unconscious beliefs that are holding you back from intentional manifesting. Energy work plus positivity equals you "getting stuff." These completely channeled events are your opportunity to engage directly with Jeshua, with your questions guiding the conversation. Their teachings leave you with concrete understanding and actionable steps that are easy to implement.

Classes with Jeshua (partial list, see website for current schedule):

Unfoldment Into Channeling –
Your Gateway to Intuitive Development

Jeshua Is. They are Consciousness. They are Infinite Intelligence. They are Source Beings. Their guidance always produces results because they are the Teachers—they explain why. They know how our minds work, where you are in your development, what your skills are, and what your Guide wants you to know about your progress. They increase your confidence—as well as your accuracy. There is no better way to learn how to communicate with your Guide and Loved Ones than with channeled instruction. Antioch from the Jeshua Collective leads discussion topics to combine exploratory and cognitive-based learning to aid your development. They not only teach you exercises and validate your progress but also who "nonphysical Beings" are and why guidance from them is so important.

The Art of Self-Healing

Directing Energy to Self-Heal is the focus of this class. Elohim from the Jeshua Collective has created a program designed for healthy living, no matter who you are, how old you are, and what your current health status is. This life is meant to be lived happy, healthy, and prosperous. Directing Source Frequency through your etheric "grid" clears your mind and body of unconscious beliefs by a little or a lot, depending on your commitment to it. There are ways to heal and there are ways to create healing—Jeshua shows you both.

About the Author

Carol Collins, named Top 10 Women to watch by LA Weekly, is the original channel for The Jeshua Collective. Much to her surprise, her abilities spontaneously manifested in March 2019. After nine months of quiet meditation, "face-spelling" was introduced as a means of direct communication, followed by "voice-giving" (trance channeling) within a few weeks. Through her, Jeshua teaches about the Four Pillars of learning—collective consciousness, manifesting with ease, health and wellness through natural healing, and intuitive studies bringing out the natural abilities of communicating with Source in everyone—which They call The Essential Material. Carol offers private sessions with Jeshua for readings and attunements daily; retreats, and signature workshops frequently. She has been interviewed by celebrity personalities, featured in over two dozen magazines, has an extensive list of courses available in the Jeshua's Center for Intuitive Studies. In her third year of channeling Jeshua wrote eleven books through her—with more on the way. The first, Ocularity of the Mind, was released in fall 2022 and reached #1 for New Releases on its Amazon debut.

You're invited to contact and follow Carol:

    Website: www.thepittsburghmedium.com
    Email: carol@thepittsburghmedium.com
    Facebook: The Pittsburgh Medium and The Teachings of Jeshua Fan Page
    Instagram: The Pittsburgh Medium
    Peloton ID: EatLoveBike
    YouTube: The Pittsburgh Medium

www.ingramcontent.com/pod-product-compliance
Lightning Source LLC
Chambersburg PA
CBHW071415160426
43195CB00013B/1702